Ann Putnam fell onto the floor, doubled up and screaming for help.

Before anyone could come to Ann's assistance, the whole group of afflicted children were screaming and rolling on the floor and dashing themselves blindly against the benches and walls.

"She is pulling my arm," Ann Putnam was yelling, "pulling my arm and biting me because I told on her!"

At last the minister was able to raise his voice above the noise. "Turn her away!" he shouted to the constables who waited helplessly near Sarah Goode. "Turn her eyes away so that she cannot look upon them."

The Witchcraft of Salem Village

By Shirley Jackson

Landmark Books®

Random House 🏠 New York

www.randomhouse.com/teens

Library of Congress Cataloging-in-Publication Data
Jackson, Shirley, 1914–1965. The witchcraft of Salem village. SUMMARY: Describes
the social and religious conditions surrounding the Salem witch hunts, the extensive
trials and executions, and the aftermath of the hysteria. 1. Witchcraft—Massachusetts—
Salem—Juvenile literature. 2. Salem (Mass.) History—Juvenile literature.
[1. Witchcraft—Massachusetts—Salem. 2. Trials (Witchcraft)—Massachusetts—Salem.
3. Salem (Mass.)—History.] I. Title. BF1576.J3 1987 974.4'502 87-4543
ISBN: 0-394-89176-7 (trade) — ISBN 0-394-90369-2 (lib. bdg.)

Printed in the United States of America   July 2001   23 22 21 20 19 18 17 16 15
14
RANDOM HOUSE and colophon and LANDMARK BOOKS and colophon are registered
trademarks of Random House, Inc.

For my son Barry

Contents

NOTE

Salem, Massachusetts, and Salem Village, Massachusetts, were two separate places in 1692. Although only a few miles apart, they differed a good deal. Salem, where the witchcraft trials were held, was a large town, busy and active. Salem Village was a small community, self-centered and frequently almost isolated in the winter, although one of the main highways of Massachusetts ran, and still runs, past the site of Ingersoll's inn. The witchcraft cases began in Salem Village, although Salem has had to accept full responsibility. Salem Village no longer exists. Even the ghosts of George Burroughs's two wives would have trouble finding it today.

Goodwife, shortened to Goody, and Goodman were the usual forms of address during this period.

Shirley Jackson

1

THE UNEASINESS OF SALEM VILLAGE

Building a new life in a wilderness is a job for strong and heroic people. The Puritans of the Massachusetts colony had to surmount unbelievable difficulties in order to stay alive. Their first years, of course, were spent in setting up houses and clearing enough ground to plant crops.

In order to clear a space of land for farming it was necessary to plan for years ahead, and the work required a strong back and a strong faith. The trees were cut down by hand with an axe in such a manner that they would all fall inward upon one another. This was done early in the spring. The trees lay where they had fallen all summer, so that they would dry out, and in the fall they were burned. The result was a burned-over patch of land, filled with stumps and charred embers. When the embers were carted away, a crop of sorts—usually barley or corn—could be planted between the stumps, and the area used for grain for several years. Then, when the stumps were enough decayed to be drawn out by oxen and chains, the rocks must be removed. Thus, after several years, the land was ready for farming. It could be plowed and a real field of grain planted.

The Indians were a constant danger, and a man working alone in a field was easy prey for them. It was necessary for the farmers to keep weapons by them always. There had been killings by Indians around many of the small villages nearly every year, and as late as 1691 it had been nec-

2

essary for the county of Essex to establish a corps of twenty-four scouts for protection.

Although it was part of the Puritan plan for each man to have a voice in government through his standing in the church, all did not prosper equally. Some were natural leaders and gradually acquired more land and consequently more influence. Some were, unfortunately, lazy. At a Salem town meeting in 1644 it was ordered that two people be appointed every Sunday to walk about the town and take note of those backsliders who did not attend church services, or who "lye at home or in the fields without giving good account thereof." In addition, these patrols were to watch out for Indian attacks and fires.

Travel was, naturally, a hazardous and unpopular activity. Roads were not so necessary as houses and food, and the original custom was to blaze trees to show a track from one farm to another. As these tracks became paths, the underbrush was gradually cleared from them until they became wide enough to permit a horse and rider to pass. After enough traffic the path became hardened and widened until it might almost have been called a road.

Boston was the most important settlement in the colony. By 1690 it was a busy city, the center of government and education. Its people tended to be broader in their views than those in the smaller villages, although their religious discipline was almost as severe. In the smaller places, however, the church was the meeting house, the center of all village activity. In Boston there were government houses, Harvard College, shops, and taverns. People in Boston did not have to gather in the meeting house on Sunday to hear all the news, as people did in Salem Village.

By the late seventeenth century the people of the Massachusetts colony—especially in Boston—had already shown strong tendencies toward independence. Because they were so far away from England and the English government, they grew impatient with English ways. The English Book of Common Prayer had been outlawed in the Puritan church, and banishment or death was the punishment for difference of opinion over religion. Massachusetts required its officials to take an oath of allegiance to Massachusetts, but no longer were they required to take an oath of allegiance to the English government. The colony coined its own money, and arbitrated its own disputes.

In an effort to stamp out this growing feeling of independence, a new English governor named Sir Edmund Andros was sent to Massachusetts in 1686. He tried to enforce the English laws. He levied new taxes and declared that many land titles determined by the colonists were invalid, or at least doubtful until they had been confirmed in England.

When the colonists realized that their right to the land they had farmed and cleared was going to be questioned, they rebelled and put Andros into prison, where he was kept for several months until he was sent back to England. As a result, their charter as a colony was revoked, and it was necessary for Massachusetts to send some of its most important men to England in an attempt to get a new charter and establish land rights.

By the year 1692, the whole Massachusetts colony was disturbed and uneasy. In addition to the revoked charter, a calamity which affected every resident of the colony, there were rumors of war with France. The Indians still represented an immediate danger. Taxes were almost unbearably heavy, and attacks by pirates had damaged the growing commercial traffic of the colony.

In addition, the clergy were crying out against heresies and the inroads the devil had made among the people. Cotton Mather, in particular, was playing an important part in making the question of witchcraft a vital issue. Mather, a popular, passionate preacher in Boston, felt that his own war with the devil was being carried on constantly, and that the devil had marked him as a particularly desirable prey.

Cotton Mather was called in to wrestle with the devil in several cases of possession, when the devil spoke through a human body which he had entered. Mather and the possessing demons had bitter and furious quarrels, but Mather was usually victorious. He published accounts of some of his battles with the devil, citing the devil's own words and his threats against godly people, and these publications were widely circulated. People regarded Mather as a hero for doing battle personally with the devil.

In Salem Village the winter of 1692 was hard and all news brought along the dangerous lonely road from Boston was discouraging. In addition, Salem Village had its own troubles. Quarrels among its people were frequent, and there were even family feuds which had been carried on for two or three generations. Moreover, the village was getting a reputation for mistreatment of its ministers.

One minister had left the town because he was involved in constant bickering. Another minister had been almost starved out when the parishioners refused to pay the money and goods owed him. And now Samuel Parris, the only minister the people had been able to find to take their church, was supported by only half the town. The other half, although they came to church, made a point of disagreeing with the minister on all town issues. Some of the residents of Salem Village who lived close enough to other towns changed their church affiliations to the churches in those towns. Samuel Parris made efforts to reconcile the different groups in the village, but without much success. He was not a very tactful or generous man. Before he accepted the position of minister, he had insisted that the people of the town guarantee his payments. He had, in addition, asked for more than the other ministers had received.

Life in Salem Village was not easy at the best of times. Gaiety and merrymaking were regarded as irreligious, and the people of the village were somber and severe. Their lives were spent in hard work and religious observance. Even their relaxation was associated with the meeting house. On the Sabbath there was a long service in the morning, and another in the afternoon. Village residents who came from outlying farms were not able to get home between the services, and it gradually became a regular practice for the time between the services to be spent in visiting and conversation. This was the time when gossip and news were spread from one to another.

Occasionally there was a simple celebration held in the village. There were sometimes boating parties and even a hayride for the young people. Dancing was not permitted, but people enjoyed visiting one another and singing together, although of course their choice of songs was limited. They could not sing anything frivolous or any song (like so many of the songs they had left behind in England) which praised earthly love or mocked at any sacred institution.

Although many of the original settlers had been educated people, the education which the children received in Salem Village was not very thorough. It was believed that so long as the children were taught correct religious doctrine they would grow up to be good citizens. Their teaching, of course, was from the Bible, and the children were told over and over again that only the greatest piety would save them from eternal damnation.

The Puritans did not celebrate Christmas or Easter, because they felt that these holidays derived from pagan ideas and were not truly religious. The occasional holidays from school were given for a practical purpose, such as getting in the harvest. Any little girl who was caught making or playing with a doll would have been punished and taken to Mr. Parris for a long, serious talking-to. The Puritans thought that toys were in general frivolous and time-wasting, and that dolls in particular were harmful. Witches were supposed to use dolls and small copies of people to work magic.

Twice a week, on Sunday and on Wednesday, the children accompanied their parents to the meeting house. There they sat on hard benches and listened to Mr. Parris's three-hour sermons, which always warned them of the extreme caution they must use against temptation. Of course, Mr. Parris knew the names of everyone in the village, and any child who wriggled, or fell asleep, or showed signs of impatience, was sure of encountering Mr. Parris's displeasure.

Mr. Parris had not had any experience with witchcraft in Salem Village, although there had

10

been rumors of witches in nearby towns. One neighboring minister had dealt with a case of witchcraft simply by sending both accused and accuser back home, with instructions to behave themselves. But many people felt that this was too lenient. Had not Cotton Mather told them of the joy among the demons whenever a Puritan succumbed to temptation? Some people whispered that when a minister was that gentle with the devil, it might mean that his secret feelings were much too sympathetic toward the forces of evil. Clergymen, they said, had been known to be witches before. Much of this gossip died away naturally, but people did not forget the incident.

Moreover, this incident demonstrated an attitude toward witchcraft which has contributed enormously to every witchcraft epidemic in history. Anyone who defended or sympathized with or said a good word for a witch was automatically suspected. It was felt that no one would help a witch without a good reason, and the reason could only be that the suspect's defender was also in league with the devil. It is this attitude which makes it so difficult for intelligent and thoughtful people to stop a great popular hatred like the hatred toward the witches.

THE DEVIL
COMES CLOSER

In Salem Village in the early days of the year
1692, people were gossiping about the charter,
about the Indians, and about the scarlet bodice
that Bridget Bishop had made for herself. Everyone thought that Mr. Parris should be chided for
permitting his West Indian slave to wear a colored turban, but no one seemed to be paying
much attention to what the younger girls of the
village were doing.

A group of girls, ranging in age from nine to nineteen, had formed an informal club. Nearly every day they would gather in the big cheerful kitchen of Mr. Parris's house to talk to Tituba, the West Indian slave who wore the bright turban. If any of their elders noticed this, or cared, it must have seemed to them that the girls could get into very little trouble in the home of the minister of the town. They were quiet and seemed well behaved, and perhaps the elders thought that Tituba was instructing them in the various duties of housework and cooking.

Little Elizabeth Parris was the youngest, and the older girls disliked having her tagging along. She was only nine years old, and her cousin Abigail Williams, who lived in the Parris house, was eleven. Abigail's closest friend in the village was Ann Putnam, who was twelve. Although Ann was always very polite and sweet when grownups were around, she could be very rude and cruel to other children. Elizabeth Parris, and even some of the older girls, were afraid of her. Mary Walcott, for instance, seemed to copy whatever

Ann did, even though Mary was five years older. And Elizabeth Hubbard and Elizabeth Booth and Susannah Sheldon, who were all seventeen and eighteen years old, let Ann order them around just as she pleased. The only one who ever stood up to Ann was Mercy Lewis, and even she never dared quarrel openly with Ann.

All of these girls spent as much time as possible in the Parris kitchen. Sometimes the older ones even sneaked in for a few minutes when they were supposed to be running an errand or finishing up their work at home. Several of the older girls worked as servants in village homes, and of course it was even more difficult for them to come. But somehow they all managed to spend a good deal of time in the Parris kitchen with Tituba.

Mostly, Tituba told them stories. Although she had been brought up in the Spanish West Indies in what the Puritans considered a heathen voodoo faith, Tituba had been converted to Christianity, and was now as sincere a churchgoer as any of the rest of the villagers. Somehow, though, when Tituba told the girls about Adam in the

15

Garden of Eden, or Noah and the ark, the stories sounded different, more interesting than when Mr. Parris told them from the pulpit. Tituba did not want to do these girls any harm, but she could not forget the magic and superstition she had known in her youth, and slowly the girls began to learn more about magic than they did about Noah.

Then the girls began to realize that what they were listening to was wrong by all the teachings of their church. Several of them, particularly little Elizabeth Parris, even felt that they could be punished, although she probably could not have explained why she felt that she was doing what her father would have called sinning. The other girls told Elizabeth that she was silly to worry about sin when all she did was let Tituba tell her fortune from the lines in her palm. Anyway, they pointed out, it was done, and nothing could change it now.

Ann Putnam made it very clear to little Elizabeth that the other girls had no desire to get into trouble just because Elizabeth was acting like a baby. And, she warned, if Elizabeth told her father or anyone else, they would see that she regretted it for the rest of her life. Ann shook her fist in Elizabeth's face, and scowled at her horribly, and said she would do something terrible to Elizabeth if she said one single word. Elizabeth was too frightened to speak, but night after night she lay in her bed awake, wondering if she had condemned herself to eternal damnation when she let Tituba read her palm.

The other girls were excited by these forbidden games, and if they felt any fear of eternal damnation, they kept it to themselves after what had happened to Elizabeth. None of them dared to defy Ann Putnam. Besides, Tituba knew charms for catching a young man's fancy, and making hair curl, and she could tell the real meaning of dreams. The winter months were long and gloomy, and Tituba herself loved to remember the warm days of her youth, and try to forget the snow and cold wind outside. The girls went through their dreary tasks more cheerfully, thinking about the exciting fortunes Tituba had promised lay ahead for them. One of them was going to travel, another was going to have three husbands, another was going to marry a rich man, perhaps from as far away as Boston.

The January snow was heavy, and the winter, which already seemed endless, still had many long weeks to go. The people in Salem Village at last began to take notice of what the young girls were doing. It was said that some of the girls were behaving very strangely. They frequently did not answer when they were spoken to. They seemed very nervous, and cried without reason, and sometimes even fell into hysterical fits when they laughed and cried and could not be quieted. They screamed out meaningless words in their sleep. Families grew a little anxious. In spite of their stern ways, they loved their children. John Proctor, in whose family Mary Warren was a servant, told around the village that a good whipping had calmed Mary down wonderfully well. But not many people cared to try so severe a method.

Mr. Parris was particularly worried about his

little girl. Even though many people around the village disliked Mr. Parris and said that he was cruel and vain, no one could deny that little Elizabeth was very dear to him. He was almost broken-hearted when she woke up at night, in terrible fear, and called for him to help her fight off the terrible creatures she saw beside her bed. When he picked her up, she did not recognize him, but tried to escape from his arms. She seemed always afraid of some danger which only she could see. Tituba, too, dearly loved the child and sat before the kitchen fire crying. Elizabeth refused the dainty little meals Tituba made for her, and said that Tituba was trying to poison her. During the day the child seemed half-asleep most of the time. She lay beside the window for hours at a time, staring out at nothing, and then roused suddenly to cower back and scream in fear at the invisible phantoms which she thought were threatening her.

Everyone in town heard about it when Mr. Parris at last called in Dr. Griggs. Elizabeth must be very sick indeed, they thought. And all over the village the other girls whispered to one another that Elizabeth might even be dying and that—even worse—she might be going to tell about the games in the Parris kitchen, which now began to seem so much worse than they had before.

Dr. Griggs was an honest, well-meaning man, but he knew no more about medicine than any other doctor of the time. After he had examined Elizabeth and listened to her wild talk of phantoms at her bedside, he looked very grave. Mr. Parris took his arm and led him from the room.

"Tell me, Doctor," said Mr. Parris in great anxiety, "what ails the child?"

The doctor looked away. He could not meet Mr. Parris's worried eyes, and at last he said slowly, in a troubled voice, "The child is afflicted, Minister, and it seems to me that it can only be by witchcraft."

The news was all over town as though witchcraft indeed had carried it. Elizabeth Parris had been bewitched. Some evil person, working with the powers of the devil, had sent deliberate suffering to the child. This was worse than any kind of plague or illness. There was a witch in the village. The phantoms which frightened Elizabeth Parris were clearly the work of magic. People began to wonder about Mr. Parris's enemies in the town. Had one of them taken this method of getting even with the minister?

By nightfall, however, it was being told that Ann Putnam, too, was bewitched. When she heard the news about Elizabeth Parris, she screamed out and fell onto the floor as though she had been struck down. Now she was sitting on a bench in her father's house, shivering with fear. Many of the people of the village went to the Putnam house to see Ann and wonder at her horrible state. The diagnosis of witchcraft had been a lucky thing for the girls. It meant that now no one was going to ask Elizabeth questions which would lead to a confession of the goings-on in the Parris kitchen. Perhaps the idea that they were bewitched would save the girls from punishment if the truth did come out.

By the next day the people of the village had even more cause to be frightened. Mercy Lewis was bewitched, and so was Mary Warren. Nor were they the only ones. Abigail Williams and Mary Walcott and Elizabeth Hubbard and Susannah Sheldon and Elizabeth Booth were all falling into fits just like Elizabeth Parris. They were screaming that they saw nightmarish figures, and that they were being pinched and pushed by invisible and unknown hands.

Once witchcraft had been named, Mr. Parris, Mr. Putnam, and the other senior men of the village were all convinced that some person was purposely tormenting these girls. John Proctor remarked once again that a good whipping had worked wonderfully well with Mary Warren. No one smiled at him now, for things had become serious.

It seemed to Mr. Parris that prayer might be of some assistance, so he invited ministers from neighboring parishes and towns to gather with him. While they were assembled solemnly, devoting their prayers to the aid of the unfortunate children, little Elizabeth burst into the room, followed by her cousin Abigail. The two children crashed through the group of ministers, knocking over furniture, shouting aloud through the prayers, and badly frightening the visitors.

Later in the day, others of the afflicted girls were brought to Mr. Parris's house in the hope that the presence of the other ministers might comfort them. Instead, the girls managed to convince the ministers that they had with their own eyes seen the torments of the demons, and had come almost face to face with the devil himself. The girls shouted and yelled meaningless words, rolled on the floor, and could not be held still. Abigail even dashed into the fireplace and scattered burning embers around the room. The visiting ministers looked at one another in horror. Cotton Mather had described demons as acting in this manner. The other ministers joined with Mr. Parris in a hasty prayer, and fled.

It fell then to Mr. Parris to discover the person in his parish who was doing this harm. No one doubted that the torments of the girls were the result of the activities of some living person in league with the devil. The only question was who?

In his own study, where he wrote his sermons, Mr. Parris questioned the sick girls. In spite of their cries and interruptions he explained to them that if they could succeed in identifying the person who was practicing witchcraft upon them, the whole village would be saved from a danger which might otherwise destroy it. He told them how one person could, with the devil's help, demolish a whole town. He told them that the actual safety of the village depended upon their attempting to recognize the witch who hurt them. Kindly and gently, with the important men of the village standing anxiously by, Mr. Parris asked the girls again and again if they knew who afflicted them.

Ann Putnam sat silently while Mr. Parris spoke. Her father and her uncles were watching her, and she stared without speaking into the fire. Finally, Mr. Parris turned to her and said, "Tell us, if you can, who has afflicted you thus."

Ann seemed not to hear, and yet, when Mr. Parris repeated his question, she stirred and looked up at him trustingly. "I am not afflicted," she said sweetly. "I am very well, Minister." Then, with a horrible scream, she threw herself onto the floor, so that Mr. Parris had to catch her quickly to keep her from hurting herself against the furniture. When he lifted her, she lay stiff in his arms with her teeth clenched tight and her eyes staring. All of those watching saw tooth marks on her arms, as though she had been bitten, and she said wildly, "Please, Minister, tell them to leave me alone. I will never put my name to the devil's book, no matter how they hurt me."

Horrified, Mr. Parris turned to the other girls and demanded if any of them knew who was hurting Ann. Mercy Lewis said that she was not sure, but she thought she had seen someone come to Ann and bite her arm. The other girls joined in. They were all fairly sure that they had seen something of the sort.

When Ann opened her eyes again and looked around as though in surprise, Mr. Parris again asked her if she knew who had come to her and hurt her.

"I cannot be sure," Ann said, as though reluctantly. "I *thought* I saw someone."

Mr. Parris and the others pressed her to name the person she thought she saw. Ann was unwilling. She said she did not want to injure an innocent person if she was wrong, and if she was right the witch would only come after her again and hurt her even more. Again the other girls agreed. The witch, they said, was dangerous. They did not dare name her for fear of further punishment. Mr. Parris and the other men promised them every possible protection, and Mr. Parris offered a fervent prayer in their defense. During Mr. Parris's prayer the witch forced the girls to yell so loudly that frequently the minister's words could not be heard. And when Mr. Parris, at the end of his prayer, grew more than usually eloquent, it was necessary for two of the men to hold Ann Putnam to keep her from throwing herself bodily at the minister.

Elizabeth Parris was almost asleep in one corner of the room. When at last her father finished his prayer and turned in despair to take his small daughter into his arms, she stirred sleepily and murmured, "Tituba."

"Tituba?" repeated Mr. Parris, turning to look at the other girls. "Is it Tituba?"

"Tituba!" shouted Ann, and then the others followed. "Tituba," they said. "She has done this."

Before Mr. Parris could take more than a step toward the door, Mercy Lewis raised her voice. "She is not alone!" Mercy cried out through the clamor. "There are others with her. I see Goody Osburn, too."

"And Sarah Goode!" someone shouted. And then they called out, all together in a fearful racketing confusion, "Sarah Goode! Sarah Osburn! Tituba!"

They could not have chosen better. Sarah Goode was a woman whose reputation was already doubtful. She was poor and acted half crazy as she wandered with her ragged children from door to door, begging food and shelter and cursing those who denied her. Most of the villagers dreaded the sight of Sarah Goode and her pack of children, who were suspected of stealing what they needed when they were refused help.

Sarah Osburn was, on the other hand, a respectable woman, but one who had acquired the reputation of being strange. She spent a large part of her time sick in bed, and everyone knew her for a cross, disagreeable old woman whose house was always in disorder. Although Salem Village was a proper village, with its houses and individual properties, there were outlying farms which still came within the village limits, and Sarah Osburn lived on such a farm. The people from these farms attended the village meeting house, and sometimes came miles on horseback in order to do so. Such a journey into the village was not to be undertaken casually, and frequently the only contact the village inhabitants had with these distant neighbors was in the meeting house and in the social gatherings that filled the time between sermons. Consequently, most of what the villagers knew about their distant neighbors was derived from these weekly meetings and from stories brought back by visitors to the farms.

Tituba lived in the village, in the house of Mr. Parris. Sarah Osburn lived on an outlying farm, and Sarah Goode lived wherever she could find shelter. It is certain that the bewitched girls knew a good deal about these women from local gossip—a vice heartily condemned by their church. Their mothers had surely talked among themselves of the shiftlessness of Sarah Goode, and the slovenliness of Sarah Osburn, and had perhaps even told one another that such behavior was the devil's handiwork. Certainly the people of the village, shocked and horrified at the fact of witchcraft, were not at all astonished to find out who the first witches were.

It is possible that the girls did not really mean to accuse their friend Tituba. The mention of her name could have been a last attempt to explain the strange position in which they found themselves.

On February 29, 1692, warrants were issued against Sarah Goode, Sarah Osburn, and Tituba. It was felt that a crime so dangerous must be accepted as a public responsibility, and so four of the most important men in the village signed their names to the complaint against the witches.

Thomas Putnam was one of these. He was the father of Ann, and the parish clerk. Edward Putnam, his brother, who also signed the complaint, was a deacon. Joseph Hutchinson, another signer, was generally regarded as one of the wisest men in the village, as well as one of the wealthiest. And Thomas Preston, the fourth of the men to sign, was a representative of one of the great local landowning families. The family to which Preston belonged was also one which had shown great opposition to Mr. Parris, so Thomas Preston's signature upon the first warrant showed the people that no private feuds would be allowed to stand in the way of destroying this great danger.

Today it seems strange that no one made the slightest attempt to stop this epidemic at the very beginning. A few people advised caution, and suggested that the village must not judge too hastily, but wise words were ignored in the general fear of witchcraft. The general political tension in the colony, combined with the superstitious fear of the devil's power, exploded almost at once into uncontrollable hysteria.

Mr. Parris is generally believed to be largely responsible for the witchcraft trials. He was badly frightened, and worried because his own daughter was one of the tormented girls. Moreover, he probably realized that the people would turn to their church as a protection against the devil, and that he would become a very important man if he was able to defeat the devil in his own village. Therefore, instead of trying to quiet the general fear, he seemed to be working hard to increase it. His sermons were full of fury against the witches, and he was constantly found in prayer over the afflicted girls. Perhaps he saw himself as a second Cotton Mather, battling personally with the devil. He refused to do anything at all to restrain the afflicted girls, and they wandered freely about the village like a kind of sideshow, giving performances whenever they had an audience.

The people of Salem Village did not understand clearly what was happening, but they knew it was something dreadful. They saw a group of girls whom they had known all their lives acting like maniacs. Everything seemed strange and different. The people's first thought was to protect themselves and their families, and yet at the same time everyone was excited, too. Nothing like this had happened in the village before, and it was with a kind of fearful pride that they realized that their little village had been chosen to resist the great forces of darkness.

Mr. Parris and the ministers he called in to help him repeated endless challenges against the devil. Each member of the church knew that these challenges included him. Each man saw his neighbor frightened and so became more frightened himself. No one dared leave the only protection offered the people—the protection of Mr. Parris and their church. Eventually they came to believe that if they worked together wholeheartedly and without mercy, they could root out the evil already growing among them. No one dared hesitate.

There are many theories about the behavior of the girls themselves. Ann Putnam was the ringleader, and she was a nervous, imaginative child, full of strange fancies and delusions. She may actually have convinced herself that she was being tormented by witches. On the other hand, she may have seen that pretending to be tormented was a wonderful way of attracting attention. Many years later Ann was to say, asking public penance, "I did it not out of any anger, malice, or ill will."

Originally, the only girls bewitched were those who had gathered around Tituba. Two or three others joined them later. All of these girls had one thing in common. They were willing, originally, to risk severe displeasure and punishment for the sake of the excitement offered by Tituba and her magic. Moreover, their forbidden amusements could not have been kept secret much longer, because of the growing nervousness among the weaker girls. If they had not fortunately become bewitched just in time, they would all have been in very serious trouble. Certainly they did not at first expect to get anyone else into trouble, or do any harm. They were most unwilling to put a name to any witch when their afflictions began. It was only after the most searching questioning by Mr. Parris and the other ministers that it began to be clear that the girls must either name a witch or become objects of deep suspicion themselves.

3

A BLACK MAN FROM BOSTON

For most of the people in Salem Village this was the first time the devil had come close enough to be recognized, but everyone knew the proper actions to be taken. The witch must be examined in the correct legal manner and questioned with regard to her crimes. These crimes were supposedly the cause of her arrest. In the first cases, the accusation was the tormenting of the girls. In later cases, the witches were accused of a wide variety of demonic acts, ranging from destruction of property to actual murder. In reality, however, it was assumed that all that was necessary was proving the prisoner a witch. That would demonstrate that she had committed the crimes.

If possible, the witch must be made to confess that she had deliberately chosen to follow the ways of the devil, and that she had signed his great black book, in which were recorded the names of all the devil's people. The more information she could give, the better, particularly with regard to the names of other witches. Also, if she described the celebrations and meetings she attended, and the laughing and singing the devil encouraged, then it would show godly folk that such gaiety was the direct road to damnation.

The preliminary examination upon suspicion of witchcraft was an attempt to determine whether there was enough evidence to hold the witch in prison to wait for a formal trial and a sentence. If the preliminary examination showed that there was not enough evidence to justify holding her for trial, she was released. Of course, there was always the possibility that she might be arrested again.

Since the judges could obviously not get hold of a copy of the devil's big black book, they had no way of knowing who had signed it and who had not. If the witch confessed, fine. If she could not be persuaded to confess, the court had to rely on various other forms of evidence which were traditionally believed to be proof of witchcraft. The most important of these was what was called spectral evidence. If the specter, or ghost, or spirit, or apparition, or vision which resembled a person appeared to another person who was afflicted by witchcraft, it was regarded as absolute proof that the first person was a witch, whether she knew it or not. The judges reasoned that only a person in league with the devil could send a ghostly form to trouble innocent people. And if the person accused protested that she knew nothing about it, and had no acquaintance whatsoever with the devil, that was even worse. It was assumed that her apparition had signed the devil's book for her.

Sometimes when particularly ignorant or foolish people were accused and heard that their spirits had been doing witchcraft without their knowledge, they were frightened enough to believe that the accusation was true. Then they were encouraged to think back as carefully and closely as possible for some small incident which might show that without knowing it they had encountered and encouraged the devil. Dreams were very popular for this. A violent nightmare, particularly one about being chased by some indescribable monster, was the clearest possible indication that the devil was after you. Many confessions hinged on such stories. One or two of the witches said sadly that if they had only realized what their bad dreams really meant, they would have hurried to the minister for protection.

There were many other ways of proving witchcraft. Since witches were supposed to be able to do magic, the possession of anything that looked like a magical appliance was very good proof. A doll, for instance. Images of the human form were specifically forbidden by the Bible. A skillful witch could fashion a rough little doll to represent an enemy, and cause the enemy great harm merely by hurting the doll. This is called image magic, and it is found in some form in every system of magical belief. It was present in Tituba's voodoo background and in the Puritan Bible teachings. Among Tituba's people it was no doubt believed that an enemy could hurt you if he managed to secure clippings from your fingernails, or a lock of your hair, or even if he caught your shadow or your footprints under the proper circumstances.

Even words could be evidence. A threat might be remembered and brought out against an accused person. Witches were able to put curses on people, and a witch who wished evil to someone was of course responsible when that person came to harm. A suspected witch in England was found guilty because, quarreling with a neighbor, she said some words under her breath, and not ten minutes later her neighbor's wagon went over a rock and broke an axle.

So the people of Salem Village felt that they had many ways of determining whether the three women named by the afflicted girls were actually witches. In England and Europe witches were tortured to make them confess, but the people of

Salem Village would have thought themselves barbarians if they had used any such methods. The principal evidence was that of the afflicted girls, whose group was soon enlarged to include several married women. The most important of these was the mother of little Ann Putnam—Ann Putnam senior. In spite of the fact that these grown women were included, the group was always referred to as "the afflicted children."

On the first day of March 1692, no work was done in the homes or fields of Salem Village. Early in the morning, as though it were a Meeting Day, the people dressed in their best. They gathered excitedly around the big house of Nathaniel Ingersoll, which was half dwelling, half inn, and the main center of gossip and news in the town. It had been assumed by everyone that the examination of the witches would surely be held at Ingersoll's. By early morning almost the entire population of the village was assembled. The grownups were talking anxiously and quietly together; the children were running off down the road and back again, with wild excited shouts. The afflicted children were in a room of the inn, attended by parents and relatives.

Before anyone had time to grow really impatient, some children came running down the road, shouting that the magistrates were in sight. The people watched in wonder as the procession came nearer. The two magistrates were dressed in all the elaborate finery which belonged to their high office, and with them rode the constables and most important men of the village, all dressed in their best, and all looking very serious and important.

The magistrates were people of importance and prestige in the Salem Village neighborhood. It was considered a great honor to the whole village that these men had consented to conduct the examination of the witches. Both of them were prominent men in the Massachusetts colony, and their dignity and authority awed the villagers. John Hathorne, the presiding magistrate, was a handsome man, though cruel and narrow-minded. Jonathan Corwin, the second magistrate, was less proud and less handsome. But he was an ambitious man, happy to be the center of so much attention.

Both Hathorne and Corwin were men of education and intelligence. They both, however, believed firmly in the power of the devil and in witchcraft. They saw their duty clearly in Salem Village. They were to discover evidence of witchcraft, to examine and try witches. They would not deliberately condemn anyone who was innocent. They would not accept false evidence. They would assure every accused person a fair trial. But it was well known that the devil loved to confuse and tangle those who sat in judgment, and Hathorne and Corwin were both determined that they were not going to be misled by any devilish tricks. If the devil tried to come to the assistance of his people during these trials, he was going to find that Hathorne and Corwin were more than a match for him.

The parade of legal might drew rein before Ingersoll's inn, and it was immediately apparent that there was not going to be room for everyone inside. A brief consultation took place among the magistrates, Mr. Parris, and several visiting ministers. Mr. Parris was of the opinion that this was a matter of enough serious heavenly importance to be conducted in the meeting house. He overruled the doubts of the others about the fitness of holding a trial in a house of religion. And so off to the meeting house paraded the magistrates, the village leaders, the afflicted children and their companions, and, finally, the rest of the population of the village. They crowded hastily into the meeting house.

The magistrates were seated at a long table placed directly in front of the pulpit, where they would face the people in the audience. The afflicted children were allowed to sit in the front row. Between the magistrates and the afflicted children a space was left, where the prisoners were to stand.

When everything was quiet, and everyone had settled down, Mr. Parris mounted his pulpit and prayed for the help of heaven in the examination to come. When he was finished, Constables Locker and Herrick brought in the three accused women. Sarah Goode was defiant and pulled away from Constable Locker because he held her too roughly. She glared at the judges and the assembled people. Sarah Osburn was frightened, and Tituba was confused. Although all three women were fairly well known to the people of the village, the spectators now craned their necks and tried to stand on the benches to catch a glimpse of them. Because of the general pushing to see the prisoners, the magistrates directed the constables to bring the three women up onto the platform beside the magistrates' table so that they could be clearly seen.

The first evidence was given by the constables. They reported that the three accused, and their homes and possessions, had all been thoroughly searched, and no sign of magic or fiendish property had been found. The prisoners were then asked whether they pleaded guilty or not guilty, and all three said firmly that they were not guilty. Sarah Goode was the first to be examined. During her examination Tituba and Sarah Osburn were taken back to Ingersoll's inn to wait.

The examination of Sarah Goode, which is preserved in legal records of the time, is a clear example of the kind of "fair" trial given the witches. Since Sarah Goode was the first person accused in Salem Village, the trial was a novelty to both audience and accused, and no one was quite sure how to behave. Sarah Goode was very angry and very frightened. She was a poor, ignorant woman who had not been very faithful in her churchgoing, and she was almost speechless before the fierce gaze of the magistrates. Moreover, so many important people seemed to think she was a witch that she was almost persuaded that they were right.

When she looked around from her place on the platform, the faces she saw were faces she had known all her life. Many of these people had been unkind to her, and she had quarreled with many of them. She knew that most of the people in Salem Village disliked her, but now she could see that they were afraid of her. It was almost enough to make her afraid of her own self. On her right was the long table, and the magistrates and clerks and ministers leaning over it to look at her. Below her, in the front row, she could see little Ann Putnam, fresh and neat and clean, sitting beside her mother. She had known Ann since the child was born, and her mother, too. Ann Putnam senior had once driven her from the door when she came begging food. There was little Betsy Parris, and Mercy Lewis, and Mary Warren, all of them seeming so honest and obedient.

"Sarah Goode," said Magistrate Hathorne at last. He leaned farther forward to watch her carefully, and the courtroom was very quiet. "Sarah Goode," he said gravely, "what evil spirit have you familiarity with?"

Sarah Goode looked around helplessly and tried twice to speak before she could make the word come out. "None," she said finally.

"Have you made no contracts with the devil?"

The people in the meeting house shivered and moved closer together, thinking of how Goody Goode, right up there on the platform, might have seen and even talked with the devil himself.

"No," said Sarah Goode. But no one believed her.

"Why do you hurt these children?" Judge Hathorne demanded sternly.

"I do *not* hurt them," said Sarah Goode with

indignation. She was frightened and confused when they talked about the devil, but she knew Ann and Betsy and Mary and Mercy and the rest so well that their accusations only made her angry. "I scorn it," she said contemptuously.

"Then whom do you employ to do it?" Judge Hathorne asked. "To hurt the children?"

"I? I employ nobody."

"What creature, then? If not a person, what creature?"

"No creature," said Sarah Goode. "I am falsely accused."

"Have you made a contract with the devil?"

"No," said Sarah Goode flatly, looking Judge Hathorne in the eye as she spoke.

Judge Hathorne shook his head and whispered to Judge Corwin. Then Judge Hathorne turned to look down upon the afflicted children in the front row. "Children," he said gently, "look here on Sarah Goode, and tell if she is the person who hurts you."

Gravely, Ann and Betsy and Mary and Mercy and Abigail and the rest turned their eyes to look at Sarah Goode. Then, so suddenly that the meeting house was thrown into a wild clamor, Ann Putnam screamed and leaped to her feet and then fell onto the floor, doubled up and screaming for help.

Before anyone could come to Ann's assistance, the whole group of afflicted children were screaming and rolling on the floor and dashing themselves blindly against the benches and walls. The audience was in dreadful confusion. A woman fainted and her husband almost had to fight his way to the door to carry her outside. Everyone was anxious to get as far away from the witch as possible.

"She is pulling my arm," Ann Putnam was yelling, "pulling my arm and biting me because I told on her!"

The others, rolling and kicking so madly that it was impossible to get close enough to hold them, cried out that Goody Goode was pinching them, scratching them, biting and pushing.

"She is going to bite Mary Warren," Mercy called out, and Mary Warren shrieked and gasped that she was bitten.

The magistrates stood up behind their table to

watch in shocked silence. Meanwhile, Sarah Goode stood on the platform, forgotten, her face white and her eyes staring, too frightened to move. At last Mr. Parris, accustomed to making himself heard in his own meeting house, was able to raise his voice above the noise. "Turn her away!" he shouted to the constables who waited helplessly near Sarah Goode. "Turn her eyes away so that she cannot look upon them." The constables seized Sarah Goode's arms and whirled her around so that her back was toward the afflicted girls, and like magic there was quiet again.

All over the meeting house people stood, hesitating in the act of flight. Judge Hathorne still had his mouth open. The afflicted girls got up off the floor, dusted off their clothes, and went back to their seats. They were no longer neat and clean. Their clothes were torn and their faces tearstreaked, their hair was tangled, and people near them could see the marks of teeth on their arms. Sobbing a little still, they sat down in the front row again.

"She has bitten them," someone whispered. And the words ran like a wind through the meeting house. "There is blood on Mary Warren's arm. She has bitten them."

"Sarah Goode," Judge Hathorne cried out, "do you not see *now* what you have done? Why do you not tell us the truth? Why do you thus torment these poor children?"

"I do not," said Sarah Goode helplessly. "I do not torment them."

"How came they thus tormented?"

"What do I know?" Sarah Goode was more bewildered than anyone else in the meeting house. Here was surely witchcraft, and yet she *knew* she had done nothing. She had only stood here amazed while the children were tormented, so who *could* have done it?

"Who was it, then," asked Judge Hathorne softly, "that tormented the children?"

Shaking her head in wonder, Sarah Goode said at last, "It was Osburn." It must have been, she was thinking, because *she* had not done it. It must be that Osburn and Tituba were tormenting the children. "It was Osburn," Sarah Goode said, nodding her head.

* * *

This was the examination of Sarah Goode. It was perfectly clear to the judges and to the people that she was guilty. She had bitten the children right before their eyes. When she was turned around, the children were quiet. The children saw her apparition when it came to attack them, and recognized it clearly. No further proof was necessary. It was a good thing, too, that Witch Goode had been frightened into naming her accomplice, Osburn. Indeed, the devil was going to find that he had picked the wrong place when he decided to settle in Salem Village.

The people in the meeting house sat back comfortably as Sarah Goode was taken back to prison and Sarah Osburn brought in. Because of the horrible experience with Sarah Goode, this witch was placed so that she could not look down at the children without turning entirely around to do so, and the constables stood ready to catch her if she tried to move.

The case against Sarah Osburn had grown much stronger since Witch Goode had incriminated her. Otherwise, it was much the same case. Her spirit had tormented the afflicted children.

No one liked her much. She had at one time been a respectable and well-to-do woman, but after the death of her first husband she had married again, but had not been happy with her second husband. People began to wonder, now, about the death of her first husband. Could it have been due to witchcraft? And was her second husband afraid of her because of it? Anyone who could bewitch a man to death would surely feel few scruples about tormenting a group of young girls. Wild speculations began to fly about the audience, and people whispered to one another things they never before had dreamed of saying—cruel, unprovable things which would not have occurred to them a week earlier.

Probably Sarah Osburn was as ill mentally as physically. She was a semi-invalid and did not come often into the village. She frequently missed service in the meeting house. She was an unhappy, lonely woman, and in her confusion she made a bad appearance in the court. It was reported by the constables who came to arrest her that she had been surprised at the accusation and had said ruefully that she was more likely to be bewitched herself than to be a witch. When Judge Hathorne, in great excitement, asked her what she could possibly mean by such a statement, poor Sarah Osburn could only answer truthfully, "I was one time frighted in my sleep, and either saw or dreamed I saw a thing like a man all black, which did pinch me and pull me by the hair."

Before the judge could speak, a nervous stirring began in the audience. Finally a woman rose and said, red-faced, that she wanted to tell something on Sarah Osburn. The judge bowed graciously and bade the woman speak, and the woman, with much hesitation and correction from her husband and her friends, finally explained that Goody Osburn had long ago told her this story about the black man and the dream. Goody Osburn had also told her, the woman said, that she would never believe that lying spirit again.

"Well," Judge Hathorne said, and turned to Sarah Osburn. "Now," he continued, "what lying spirit *was* this that you would not believe again?"

"It was a voice," said Sarah Osburn miserably.

"I told her of a voice I thought I heard, dreaming."

"What did it say to you?"

"That I should not go to meeting anymore. But I said I would go, and I did go, the next Sabbath Day."

Mr. Parris leaned over, then, and whispered in the judge's ear. "But," said Judge Hathorne, "Mr. Parris tells me that you have not been at meeting since. It must be the devil who tempts you to stay away from meeting."

"Alas," said Sarah Osburn, "I have been sick and not able to go. It is well known that I have been sick." She turned to appeal to the audience, moving so suddenly that the constables were not prepared. "Will no one defend me?" she cried.

But no one could hear Goody Osburn. The minute she turned and looked toward the audience, the girls in the front row were thrown again into their convulsions. They screamed and howled so loudly that no other voice could be heard. It was not until the constables had caught Sarah Osburn and wrenched her around again that quiet once more descended upon the meeting house.

"Do you see *now* how your devil defends you?" Judge Hathorne demanded of Sarah Osburn.

The evidence was complete, and Sarah Osburn was taken to prison to await trial and sentence.

Tituba had been saved for the last. After the plain drabness of the first two witches, Tituba was an exciting sight, with her dark skin and her earrings and her colored turban. In the audience people whispered to one another that they wondered that they had not perceived long ago that Tituba was a wicked creature. Now that she stood on the platform, everyone could see how strange and unusual—and of course wicked—she was. People who had seen her every day now shivered with fear.

Tituba, for her part, was perfectly ready to testify to anything that was asked of her. She had only pleaded not guilty in the first place because the others did. She did not understand more than half of what the judges wanted, but she was willing to help in any way she could, and she made it clear at once that she wanted to help. Moreover, she understood that the one thing she was *not* to testify about was the violent whipping Mr. Parris had given her to make sure that she told the truth.

"Why do you hurt these children?" Judge Hathorne asked her.

"*I* do not hurt them," Tituba said readily.

"Who is it, then?"

"The devil," said Tituba.

"Did you never see the devil?" asked the judge.

"The devil came to me," Tituba told him, "and bid me serve him."

The audience was silent, fascinated, and the afflicted children nodded to one another. The judges bent forward to listen, and Tituba continued, "There are four women who hurt the children."

Throughout the meeting house there was a sudden shocked silence. Witch Goode was one. Witch Osburn was two. Tituba was surely three. Then suddenly there was a great burst of chatter and questions and quick startled sounds as people turned to look upon one another in fear. Who was the fourth witch?

"Also," said Tituba loudly, over the confusion,

"there is a tall black man from Boston who meets with them. I have seen them all."

Judge Hathorne, standing behind the platform, asked, "*When* did you see them?"

"Last night," said Tituba, "at Boston. There are four women and one man. They hurt the children, and they tell me if I will not hurt the children *they* will hurt *me*."

The only people quiet in the meeting house were the afflicted girls, who smiled at one another as though this were no more than they had expected. Judge Hathorne had to stop his questioning until order was restored in the meeting house.

When it was quiet enough for Tituba to continue, she went on to say that she had four times been visited by an apparition like a great black dog. This dog spoke to her and demanded that she serve him as a convert to evil. When she was afraid, the dog changed to a man and threatened to hurt her. And when she was too afraid to answer him, he began to speak kindly and offered her a yellow bird as a gift, which she refused.

"And," Tituba added, "he told me he had more pretty things that he would give me if I would serve him."

"What were those pretty things?" the judge demanded eagerly. Pretty things were not usual in Salem Village, and the audience waited tensely.

But Tituba only shook her head and said sadly, "He did not show me them."

She had seen two cats, though, she said. One of them was black and one was red. And the previous night the four witches and the black man from Boston had pulled and hauled her to the Putnam house, where they made her pinch little Ann.

Ann Putnam confirmed this. She had certainly been tormented the night before by Tituba and Goode and Osburn and—now that she thought of it—by a black man from Boston, and *two* other witches.

The other afflicted children joined in. Some of them had seen the black man from Boston and Tituba and Goode and Osburn. And almost all of the children now recalled that they had seen two mysterious witches wrapped in shawls whom they did not recognize. However, it was generally agreed that the black man from Boston was directing the others.

Apparently no one at the time questioned how they all knew that the black man was from Boston, but they were all quite positive on this point. The fact that the black man came from Boston seemed to be positive proof of his wickedness.

Judge Hathorne, eager to secure all possible information from this ready source, asked Tituba how she and the other witches—not to mention the gentleman from Boston—traveled from place to place to torment the children.

"We ride upon sticks," Tituba told him.

"Do you go through the trees or over them?" inquired the judge with interest.

But Tituba did not know. "We see nothing," she said, "but are there presently."

Tituba also said that Sarah Goode had gotten one of the yellow birds from the generous stranger, but that Sarah Osburn got a thing with a head like a woman, and two legs and wings.

At this moment Abigail Williams shouted out that this was true. Only the day before she herself had seen this creature, with its head and wings, and while she watched, it had turned into Goody Osburn.

When Tituba announced that Sarah Goode had sent a wolf to bother Elizabeth Hubbard, Elizabeth jumped up and said that was true. She *had* been teased and tormented by a wolf. She turned to the people around her and demanded, "Did I not say it? Did I not complain of a great wolf?" The people around her nodded and said why, yes, now that she mentioned it, they *did* remember her complaining about something like a wolf.

Tituba's evidence went on and on. No matter what was suggested to her, she agreed with enthusiasm, and every new fact was supported by the afflicted children. Information began to pile up. The witches met with the black man from Boston, who told them what to do. They traveled through the air to wherever they wanted to go, they kept yellow birds and cats and strange-headed monsters. They tormented the children because the children told on Goode and Osburn. Worst of all, Tituba and the children insisted over and over again, there were still two witches unidentified. No one was safe until these two were caught.

A child living in Salem Village would have found that first day a time of excitement and fear. The children were as well aware of witchcraft as their mothers and fathers. They believed that the witches in the village were as concretely dangerous as sickness or broken bones or storms which might bring trees crashing down upon the houses. Yet, to a boy or girl sitting in the meeting house that morning, it must have seemed that this was an occasion much more interesting than the usual meeting with Mr. Parris's endless sermons. Although they would have seen the usual plain bare walls and the same people who sat listening to Mr. Parris every Sabbath, they must have been impressed by the splendid clothes of the judges upon the platform. They must have stretched their necks to see the afflicted girls sitting in the front row. If they looked to either side they would have seen sudden lines of deep worry on the faces of their mothers and fathers.

Their parents had probably given them strict instructions, enforced by threats of the most dire punishments, not under any circumstances to go near the Putnam house, or the Parris house, or any places where the afflicted girls gathered together. If they met any of the girls on the street, they were to run directly home and shut the door behind them. Moreover, if by some chance they were around when Goody Goode or Goody Osburn or Tituba was being escorted to or from prison, and one of the witches should glance in their direction, the children were to hide. At once. Witches already so deeply involved might not hesitate to torment any child they saw.

Any mother certainly would only have permitted her children to come that morning because she believed that all the witches were safely under guard and could not do much harm. When it seemed, however, that there were still two witches undiscovered, and that horrible man from Boston who might come back at any minute, perhaps even walk right into the meeting house with his terrible flashing eyes and his pack of black and red cats . . .

The group of familiar faces in the meeting house must have seemed strangely altered. Hard as it was at first to believe that Goody Goode and Goody Osburn were real witches, it must have been much harder to think that there were still two people sitting there among the rest, just like anyone else (perhaps in the row ahead?) but secretly thinking of evil, perhaps even now choosing a new victim.

People looked with apprehension upon their neighbors. Goody Proctor was a godly woman, but the witchcraft had come right into her house and caught her own servant, Mary Warren. Could Goody Proctor be a witch too? Mr. Parris was a minister, but even his house was not safe. Goody Bishop was always nice to the children in the village, but the grownups said she was "willful." There sat Goody Cloyse. The Cloyses were proud people, and hard to get along with, and they had no love for Mr. Parris. Still, no one could say a wrong word about the Cloyse family. They were related to Mr. Preston, who sat upon the platform with the magistrates. Even Abigail Hobbs, whom everyone knew to be a wild creature, wandering in the woods at night, did not have the air of a witch as she sat with her hands folded in her lap, looking as worried as everyone else.

But perhaps the Cloyse family was so proud because they had gotten their land and their big houses with the devil's help. Maybe there was a reason why the witchcraft started in Goody Proctor's family. And who could tell what Abigail Hobbs met in the woods at night?

A woman leaned over to whisper to her husband. "I note that Goody Corey kept her word," she said. "She *said* she scorned to watch what she could not believe."

With the three witches back in prison, safely chained down, the villagers left the meeting house, avoiding one another, not stopping to talk. Only a few brave people dared stop by Ingersoll's inn, and they did not linger long. Almost everyone wanted to be safe at home, with doors and windows locked. The children went uneasily to bed, glancing into dark corners for the flash of unholy eyes, and the mothers and fathers sat long by the firelight. It was clear that their homes and their children were not safe until the two unknown witches were found and imprisoned.

It was also clear that it was the duty of every soul in the village to make this battle a personal one. Each family was called upon to defend its own home and to work with the ministers and magistrates to find the witches. The first thing to do was to try to remember every slightest incident, no matter how long ago, which might indicate that some person had fallen to the enemy. Every action was important, every word, every quarrel.

Mr. Parris spent long hours with the afflicted girls, sometimes working alone, sometimes assisted by ministers from neighboring parishes whom he invited to help him. When Mr. Parris was not with the girls, their parents and relatives stayed by them always. Because there were still two witches at large, the girls were still tormented, but for several days they could not see their tormentors. They moaned that their eyes were misted over to keep them from seeing, and when they tried to speak any name, they were choked and could not make a sound.

From the pulpit in the meeting house the people of Salem Village heard that they were chosen among all the people of the world to fight the devil face to face. Mr. Parris begged the people of the village to turn informer on their friends and neighbors—even, if need be, on their own families. The afflicted girls were shown off everywhere, and whenever there was enough of an audience collected, they could be relied upon to throw themselves into fits. The girls were the center of attraction everywhere, were exhibited to all visitors in the town, and were beginning to be famous in neighboring villages.

Moreover, the fits of the afflicted girls became more elaborate as time went on. At first their fits were largely a matter of yelling and rolling around on the floor. Then, as their fame and their audiences grew, they fell to biting and scratching and making horrible faces to show what agonies they were suffering. So long as people believed that they really *were* suffering, their fits were horrible to watch. It was dreadful to see a dozen girls all at once writhing with every appearance of violent pain, showing fresh bites on their arms, long red scratches on their legs, and staring wildly at the empty air, pointing to where a witch was coming at them with a knife.

One fact that made the performance even more convincing was the teamwork among the girls. When Mercy Lewis cried out that a witch was approaching Mary Warren, Mary would then scream and fall down as though struck. Sometimes they would huddle together, as though protecting one another, and then all at once fall scrambling to the ground.

For nearly two weeks after the arrest of the first three witches the excitement continued in the village. The witches were examined further, but neither Sarah Goode nor Sarah Osburn would confess to anything, and Tituba still could not reveal the names of the other two witches. On

March seventh the three witches were formally escorted to prison in Boston, with much ceremony and public attention. For a week after that the afflicted girls insisted that they could not name any new witches.

Then, guided again by young Ann Putnam, people began to murmur around the village that another witch had been discovered. Thomas Putnam was heard to observe that people who pretended not to believe in witches generally had the most to fear from an investigation. Goody Bishop remarked that *she* had heard, on the best authority, that some people were not as respectable as they seemed. It was generally agreed that refusing to attend the examinations of the witches showed a guilty conscience.

On March 19, 1692, a warrant was issued for the arrest of Martha Corey upon suspicion of witchcraft.

GREAT NOISES BY THE AFFLICTED

With the arrest of Martha Corey the entire pattern of the witchcraft fever changed. Overnight people began to realize that, rather than rooting out four or five bad characters, they were forced to deal with what seemed a widespread and deeply ingrown evil. It required some courage on the part of the afflicted girls to name Martha Corey, because she was neither defenseless nor stupid.

She was an elderly, respectable matron who was well thought of in the church, intelligent and well educated for her time. She had stayed away from the first examinations to show her disapproval of what was going on. She had declared frequently that if she did believe in witches—and she was not at all sure that she did—it would not be in witches like poor old Goody Osburn or crazy Sarah Goode.

When it was told in the village that Goody Corey had been "cried out on" by the afflicted girls, it was whispered, too, that this was only the beginning, that the circle of witches had only been partly uncovered. People began to imagine that there must be a witch society in their town, an organization known as a coven. This meant a group meeting to make plans together, rather than a few witches operating individually and without any kind of special organization.

Martha Corey was a woman of great courage. When the constables came to her house to investigate her, she laughed in their faces and told them, "I know what you are come for. You are come to talk with me about being a witch, but I am none."

The constables did not think it was entirely proper for a woman to laugh at them when they told her she was accused of witchcraft. But Martha Corey continued to laugh at them and at everyone else. Her suspicions that there were no such things as witches were easily confirmed when she saw that she herself was accused. She knew herself to be innocent, and so believed that she would be able to prove before the people and the magistrates that not only she but the "witches" before her were harmless women, falsely accused.

Unfortunately, Martha Corey did not correctly estimate the state the village had gotten itself into. She lived far enough out of town to be out of reach of common gossip, and so she had no notion of the terror the witches had inspired. She came into the village to meet young Ann Putnam face to face and force the girl to admit she was wrong. But when Goodwife Corey entered the room where little Ann lay in bed, Ann was immediately taken by such a dreadful convulsion that her parents had to push Goodwife Corey out of the room. They did this, they said, in order to save Ann's life. When Martha Corey left Ann's room and could no longer look upon Ann, the child was quiet and peaceful. Thomas Putnam lost no time in reporting this to Mr. Parris. Thus poor Martha Corey, who had been so sure that there were no witches, found herself the next to stand up in the meeting house before the magistrates.

Even then, however, Goody Corey could not take the whole thing seriously. She felt so safe in her own religious convictions and in the knowledge of her own innocence that she was sure no evidence could hold against her. Her first remark to the judges, before they could ask her a question, was "Give me leave to go to prayer."

She knew as well as the judges that witches cannot pray. And at first, every time Judge Hathorne asked her why she tormented the children, she answered only that she would tell him nothing until he allowed her a few minutes at prayer. At last Judge Hathorne grew impatient and said that she was not there to pray, but to prove she was not a witch.

"I never had to do with witchcraft since I was born," Goody Corey said calmly. "I am a gospel woman."

But at that very moment Ann Putnam shouted out, "Look, there is a black man whispering in her ear. Do you not see him?"

The other children took up the cry. All of them saw a black man whispering in Goody Corey's ear, telling her what to say.

At last Judge Hathorne asked, "What did he say to you when he whispered in your ear?"

Martha Corey smiled a little before she answered. At last she replied, "We must not believe all that these distracted children say." Her voice was patient, and she held out one hand to Judge Hathorne, as though she was sure he would understand.

Immediately, in imitation of the gesture, Ann Putnam's arms were forced out in front of her and held stiff. Then the arms of the other girls stretched out. And as long as Martha Corey held out her hand, the arms of the afflicted children were held taut and rigid, while they begged Goody Corey to let them go. When Martha Corey dropped her hand, the arms of all the children fell too.

Judge Hathorne continued, his voice severe. "Cannot you tell me what that man whispered?"

"I saw nobody," said Martha Corey.

The children then began to cry, and fall onto the floor, and ask pitifully for help. They cried that their lips were being bitten, and it was clearly seen that there was blood on their mouths. When they continued begging Goody Corey to release them, everyone could see that Goody Corey was biting her own lips, and so causing the children's lips to be bitten. When, in surprise, Martha Corey stopped biting her lips, the children were free of pain.

"We must not believe distracted persons," Goody Corey said urgently to Judge Hathorne.

But her case was already lost. If she turned even slightly toward the afflicted children, they fell screaming to the floor. If she made the smallest gesture, their arms and faces were wrenched into a distortion of the same gesture. And whenever she tried to speak, the judge shouted for her to be quiet.

"She will not come to service *next* Sabbath," Abigail Williams howled.

"I do not care," said Goody Corey flatly. She would have spoken more, but Judge Hathorne raised his voice above hers.

"Tell me the truth, will you?" he cried out. "Did you not say that the magistrates' eyes were blinded, and you would open them?" This, of all the things he had so far heard in that meeting house, was the remark which most angered Judge Hathorne. Martha Corey had said, before her examination, when she was permitted one brief prayer, that she trusted that the blindness of the judges would be removed, and they would see the truth. It was not a strange prayer under the circumstances, but Judge Hathorne interpreted it as an insult intended for himself and could not forget it. He could not possibly believe that there was any chance of *his* being wrong, and he blamed Goody Corey for hinting at such a thing.

Again and again during the examination of Goody Corey the judge returned to this unfortunate remark, and every time he referred to it, Martha Corey laughed out loud. She could see that she had wounded his vanity, and in spite of her danger she found him ridiculous. Her laughing, of course, only made things worse.

"Well?" he said to her. "You said you would open our eyes. Well?"

Martha Corey only laughed again.

The judge scowled furiously. "Do you believe you shall go unpunished?" he asked her, raging.

"I have nothing to do with witchcraft."

Someone called out from the crowd in the meeting house that Goody Corey had said she would help no one to find out witches. Judge Hathorne, who seemed aware only that Goody Corey was laughing at him, demanded again, "Did you not say you would open our eyes? Why do you not? Why do you just stand there laughing?"

"I cannot help it," said Martha Corey weakly,

laughing so that she could hardly speak. "I cannot help it."

"Is it a laughing matter to see these afflicted persons?" said the judge grimly.

"I cannot help it," said poor Martha Corey.

The afflicted children, perhaps perceiving that the judge was almost beside himself, gave him a chance to recover by putting on a demonstration of fits and convulsions that almost ended the examination entirely. By the time they were quiet again, the judge was able to proceed, and Martha Corey's examination continued. Again and again she denied having practiced witchcraft, more sober now that she saw her denials convinced no one.

Her examination filled a whole day, and to the very last she persisted in her two basic ideas: If there were witches, they were not such creatures as herself and Osburn and Goode; and secondly, the afflicted girls were poor distracted things, and no sensible person should believe a word they said.

Judge Hathorne was still smarting under Goody Corey's mockery at the end of the day, but she no longer had the strength to laugh at him. She saw clearly by then that she was on her way to prison. When the examination was over and the constables prepared to take her out, she turned once more to the people of the village who had been her friends and neighbors and said, "Ye are all against me. What can I do?"

After Martha Corey had been bound in chains and taken to prison, her husband, old Giles Corey, was brought before the magistrates. After a good deal of arguing back and forth, he was persuaded to agree that his wife had sometimes acted very oddly. The cat had been acting oddly, too, he said. So had the cow. He couldn't say that it *wasn't* witchcraft. If the judges and ministers said his wife was a witch, he was not the man to argue with them.

However, Giles Corey went home and thought about the whole matter. And the more he thought, the more he doubted. The cat and the cow had both recovered, after all. Very soon Goodman Corey showed up in the village again, to tell the judges that he had made a mistake. But before he had time to finish telling them about the cow,

Goodman Corey was in prison for witchcraft.

While Goodman Corey was at home wondering, however, the chase had gone on without him. Once everyone became convinced that a vast underground organization of witches existed, there was nothing to prevent the afflicted girls from crying out upon the highest members of the community. Some of these people, argued their neighbors, could have been secret witches for years, after all. Perhaps their very honors, their wealth, depended upon the assistance of the devil!

Rebecca Nurse, for instance, was the last person in Salem Village one would have thought of in connection with witchcraft. She and her husband were not actually members of the Salem Village church, but belonged to the neighboring congregation of Topsfield. They came to the Salem Village meeting house because it was more convenient for them, and because most of their family lived in or around Salem Village and attended that meeting house.

Rebecca Nurse and her husband had always been deeply religious, hardworking people, and perhaps there was resentment felt toward them because they had risen by their own efforts from poverty to a position of wealth and importance. Moreover, the great local family of which Rebecca Nurse was the matriarch had always been opposed to Mr. Parris's installation as minister in Salem Village. Also, there was a long history of land feuds between the villagers and the landowning faction to which the Nurses belonged. Worst of all, after the first hysterical scene in the meeting house at the examinations for witchcraft, the Nurses and allied families had pointedly withdrawn from the Salem Village church and switched to their meeting house in Topsfield.

None of this proved in any way that Rebecca Nurse was a witch, but it does suggest a reason for the violent reaction on both sides caused by her arrest. Mr. Parris and his witch-fearing villagers took old Goody Nurse from a sickbed and brought her before the magistrates. She was well over seventy years old, almost entirely deaf, and of a childlike simplicity in her religious convictions.

Thomas Preston, who signed the first witch-warrant, was a son-in-law of Rebecca Nurse. Her sisters had married into the Easty and Cloyse families. They were all people of high standing, and they rose in a fury to defend the head of their family from the shameful charges brought against her.

Her examination was a cruel affair. Goody Nurse was largely unable to hear the questions asked her and relied upon simple statements of piety to defend herself. Ann Putnam senior was her principal accuser, and during the entire examination showed a strong personal hatred for Goodwife Nurse.

There was for the first time an element of sympathy for the accused among the audience in the meeting house. Most of the people had for so long regarded Rebecca Nurse as a saint that it was difficult for them now to see her as a fiend. Mrs. Putnam did what she could to prove the charges, and the afflicted children followed her lead. They screamed, ranted, accused Goody Nurse of frightful crimes, including murder, and continued their usual dreadful imitation of the prisoner's every gesture. In spite of all this, even Judge Hathorne was touched by the pious manner of the prisoner, and for the first time showed doubt of a witch's guilt.

Again and again Judge Hathorne asked Goody Nurse to repeat her innocence, and his questions showed that he thought her falsely accused. He could not compete, however, with the influence of the accusers. At one point Rebecca Nurse, in her earnestness, lifted both hands to heaven and cried out, "O Lord, help me!" The sincerity of this appeal was immediately lost in the actions of the afflicted girls. They copied the gesture and mimicked the words, some laughing coarsely, some crying out for help to release their arms.

"I pray God clear you, if you be innocent," said Judge Hathorne helplessly.

Mary Walcott and Elizabeth Hubbard stood up in their places. One of them swore solemnly that Goodwife Nurse had come to her at night and sat upon her chest to suffocate her. The other pointed out that a black man stood, even now, whispering in Goodwife Nurse's ear and that yellow birds were flying about her head.

Rebecca Nurse was so bewildered by such accusations that she could think of nothing to say.

Then the other afflicted girls took up the cry. And Ann Putnam senior called out that Goody Nurse was not deaf, but could hear all the questions perfectly; it was the black man whispering in her ear who confused her. Goody Nurse's bewilderment and obvious ill health troubled Judge Hathorne, and he questioned her closely to discover whether she had become sick as a result of her association with the devil. When Rebecca Nurse denied any association with the devil, Judge Hathorne asked, puzzled, "Then how come you sick? Have you no wounds?"

"I have none but old age," said Goodwife Nurse with simple honesty. Wearily, she leaned her head to one side, and instantly Abigail Williams cried out that Witch Nurse was breaking Betty Hubbard's neck. Attendants with Elizabeth Hubbard begged in great alarm for Goody Nurse's head to be held up again, for the child's neck was cruelly twisted. It was not until Rebecca Nurse was forced to raise her head again that Elizabeth Hubbard gave up her agonizing position.

During the first few trials the afflicted children

had confined their demonstrations to short periods of time, and between fits they were reasonably docile. However, with the trial of Rebecca Nurse, and urged on by the malice of Ann Putnam senior, their performances became largely uncontrollable. From that time on, the examinations were conducted through the unceasing howling and acrobatics of the children. Much of the court record shows gaps in the testimony, where the questions could not be heard because of the din in the room.

The examination of Rebecca Nurse ended in a scene of the wildest confusion. The record itself was cut short, finally, because "great noises by the afflicted" prevented the reporter from hearing a word that was said. There is no doubt, however, about the result of the examination. Rebecca Nurse followed the other witches to prison.

The sensational aspects of the examination of Rebecca Nurse did much to overshadow the very brief examination which immediately followed hers. Dorcas Goode, daughter of Sarah Goode, was questioned for no more than a few minutes before being sent to join her mother in prison on suspicion of witchcraft. Dorcas occupies a unique position in the history of Salem Village witchcraft. She was not quite five years old.

The constable held little Dorcas in his arms during her examination, and Judge Hathorne made little attempt to question a child obviously unable to understand more than a fraction of what he said. Ann Putnam, Mary Walcott, and Mercy Lewis accused Dorcas of biting and choking them. When a sudden doubt swept the audience, as it did to those who glanced from Dorcas's tiny hands to the strong solid throats of Ann and Mary and Mercy, the girls screamed further. Little Dorcas was even now sticking pins into them, they yelled. And indeed the pins were found— very lightly inserted—just where the girls insisted that Dorcas had come in apparition and put them. As a result, five-year-old Dorcas joined her mother in prison.

*   *   *

Once Rebecca Nurse and Dorcas Goode had been condemned as witches, there was no reason for the afflicted girls to hesitate in naming anyone else. For a court which could condemn to prison a religious old woman and a five-year-old child upon the evidence offered by the girls could be relied upon for any absurdity. The people of the village, however, were more reluctant. The condemnation of Rebecca Nurse had worried a good many people and angered many more. No one dared to defy the court and the afflicted girls upon the question of witchcraft itself, but the family of Rebecca Nurse was aroused, and doubts of her guilt were being openly announced.

At this point the people came to meeting on the following Sunday to find that instead of Mr. Parris they were to hear a visiting clergyman named Deodat Lawson who was noted for the violence of his sermons. Mr. Lawson arrived in Salem Village with a good sermon already prepared, and within a few minutes after his arrival was visited at Ingersoll's inn by Mary Walcott, who fell into a fit at the sight of him. Her attendants explained to Mr. Lawson that the fit was caused by the extreme fear he inspired in the witches who tormented her. This horrible experience so unsettled Mr. Lawson that he retired to rewrite his sermon, to make it more emphatic. The result—which he delivered in the Salem Village pulpit on Sunday morning—was so eloquent that the sermon was printed and sold not only in Massachusetts but in the whole of New England and, finally, in England.

Mr. Lawson told the unhappy Salem Villagers in the most graphic terms that their sins had brought this great plague upon them. "Your sin will find you out," he told them. "You shall be punished with everlasting destruction from the presence of the Lord, and doomed to those endless, easeless, and remediless torments prepared for the devil and his angels. If you have been guilty, the prayers of the people of God are against you."

He begged the people to forget any weakness, any softness toward any other human being. He entreated them to give up compassion and kindness and brotherly love, and he announced at last, ringingly, that it was the Lord's command that they should turn upon one another with distrust, to seek out and destroy any upon whom the slightest suspicion rested. No one must be allowed to escape because there was a chance that he might be innocent. "And," Mr. Lawson explained, "if innocent persons be suspected, it is to be ascribed to God's pleasure."

Mr. Lawson finished his sermon on a mournful note. He greatly feared that some persons, accused and found guilty and imprisoned, might attribute their accusations to the malice of others. They might even, he said, feel some resentment toward the people who had caused them to lie in chains in prison. He earnestly prayed that such unworthy reactions would be suppressed.

Thus Mr. Lawson's instructions to the people of Salem Village and, eventually, to all New England and England, were to carry tales against their neighbors and, if possible, dig out enough evidence to accuse them. If they, in turn, reversed the process and accused the *accusers,* the latter were not to feel angry but to submit quietly and be thankful that their crimes were discovered in time.

As in all such epidemics where there is no actual disease germ to be communicated, the sickness was not controllable. Everyone was in danger, because no one, not even saintly Rebecca Nurse, has ever spent a lifetime cautiously enough to escape all criticism. One unfortunate woman was subsequently arrested because friends re-membered a quarrel she had had with her hus-band some five or six years before. Among the angry statements passed back and forth at that time were several by the husband to the effect that his wife was crazy, or bewitched, and that if he had any sense he would send her back home to her parents.

Once the accusation was made, evidence could easily be found. The witchcraft epidemic resem-bled other such great waves of fear and distrust in that proof, as such, was never required. The mere accusation was enough to destroy the per-son against whom it was aimed, and any kind of trivial incident, true or not, was considered sufficient evidence to support the accusation.

Mr. Lawson's sermon went on for more than three hours, but no one in the meeting house yawned or fidgeted. When Mr. Lawson paused for breath, the afflicted girls supplied excitement with their screaming and yelling.

Beyond the frightening effect which it had upon the congregation of Salem Village, Mr. Lawson's sermon had one other immediate result. It brought the attention of the whole country to the witchcraft cases. What had begun as a private affair in Salem Village was now seen as the responsibility of the colony as a whole, and, eventually, of the English government.

The following Sunday Mr. Parris, not to be outdone by a visiting minister, mounted his pulpit and announced a sermon of his own on the devils loose in his church. Sarah Cloyse, sister of Rebecca Nurse, smarting under her sister's unjust arrest, stood up in meeting, looked for one moment with furious indignation at Mr. Parris in the pulpit, and then turned and marched out of the meeting house, slamming the door behind her.

After a moment of shocked silence, Mr. Parris bent his head charitably in prayer. Before the week was out Sarah Cloyse joined her sister in prison.

It was then a little more than six weeks since the first signs of witchcraft in Salem Village. The villagers felt they had reason to congratulate themselves upon their prompt and thorough actions. Sarah Goode, Sarah Osburn, Tituba, Dorcas Goode, Martha Corey, Giles Corey, and Rebecca Nurse were all in prison, being held for trial. Sarah Cloyse was awaiting preliminary examination, with enough evidence coming forward to guarantee her imprisonment. Within a day or so Sarah Cloyse was joined by Elizabeth Proctor, wife of the John Proctor who had whipped Mary Warren. The principal witness against Elizabeth Proctor was to be Mary Warren herself, who had waited a long time to get even.

5

THE ROAD TO GALLOWS HILL

When the court convened again on April 11 in the Salem town meeting house, it was no longer a local court. Thanks to Mr. Lawson, to the immense publicity attending the witches going to jail in Boston, and to the rumors of accusations against people in high places, the whole colony of Massachusetts was now involved. The people of Salem Village, and the curious visitors who now began to stop off in Salem Village to see the girls afflicted by witchcraft, gathered in the meeting house in Salem town that morning and gazed with awe upon the deputy-governor of the State of Massachusetts, who was to preside at the examination. He was Thomas Danforth, Esq., representing the highest tribunal in the colony. Although this examination was still officially only a preliminary, the court included four new judges in addition to Danforth and Hathorne and Corwin. These additional judges were representatives of towns all over Massachusetts, and they were accountable to no authority except the government in England.

These seven judges were responsible for the imprisonment of more than two hundred people in a period of about five months. Their names were Thomas Danforth, James Russell, John Hathorne, Isaac Addington, Major Samuel Appleton, Captain Samuel Sewall, and Jonathan Corwin.

Sarah Cloyse and Elizabeth Proctor were brought before this august tribunal for a preliminary examination upon suspicion of witchcraft. Against them appeared a witness who had, up to now, been fairly unimportant. He was called John Indian, and he was Mr. Parris's second slave, perhaps Tituba's husband. When Tituba confessed, suspicious glances had fallen upon John, who chose a most sensible manner of preserving himself. He declared that he, too, was bewitched. However, since he did not actually join the afflicted girls in their public displays, he was left alone in the general excitement. He was enjoying himself immensely, and perhaps even profiting a little, in his position as a sort of guide around the town. Visitors to the town were glad to have John Indian show them around and point out the meeting house and the houses of the afflicted children.

Now, before the highest court in the land, John Indian appeared as the first witness in the witchcraft proceedings. He was questioned by Deputy-Governor Danforth, and testified that Goody Proctor and Goody Cloyse had tormented him. They choked him, he said, tried to force him to sign the satanic book, and pinched and bit him. At this point Sarah Cloyse cried out, "Oh, but you are a grievous liar!" She was silenced by the court.

Mary Walcott tried to testify against Sarah Cloyse, but fell into a fit before she could say more than a few words. The method now used to bring the afflicted out of a fit was one which had been found very practical in Europe and other places where witchcraft had been prevalent. The afflicted person in a fit was brought to the witch, and the touch of the witch ended the fit at once. The trials were thus being constantly interrupted by the passage back and forth of the afflicted girls being brought up to the witch for touching.

Mr. Parris asked many of the questions now, bustling and officious before the important people. His questions reveal a curious advance knowledge of what the witches were accused of doing. For instance, he asked, "Abigail Williams, did you see a company (of witches) at Mr. Parris's house eat and drink?" Up until this moment, no mention had been made of such a company, or such a celebration, but Mr. Parris seemed to know enough about it to ask the question in the manner he did. Because of this knowledge, the learned magistrates were content to sit back and let him ask a great many questions. He knew far more about all of it than they did!

Many people have wondered if perhaps Mr. Parris was not very nervous about the coming of the highest judges and took precautions to make sure that all would go smoothly. In questions like the one to Abigail Williams, the court record sounds as though Mr. Parris had coached the girls in what they were to say. Naturally he wanted his own congregation to perform as well as possible before this audience. Under his careful questioning, the girls testified to a great gathering of about forty witches. This satanic congregation, the girls said, was led by Goody Cloyse and Goody Proctor, under the supervision of a white man, a "fine, grave man, and when he came, he made all the witches to tremble." At this party the witches feasted upon the blood of their victims, provided by Goody Cloyse and Goody Proctor.

The horror of these accusations, sworn to by a slave from the West Indies and a pack of wild girls, was more than Sarah Cloyse could endure. After her one despairing cry at John Indian, she made no further attempt to interrupt, but suddenly, in the middle of the testimony, she asked weakly for water and fainted. The girls immediately shouted out, "She has gone to prison to visit her sister Nurse!" So the constables dared not bring her water or try to revive her.

The learned judges sat up on the platform during this scene, silent observers. Any one of them could have stopped the display by exerting a moment's authority. For many years afterward, Judge Sewall was to observe a day of public, personal penance for his part in the procedure. But that day he sat like the rest, horrified, aghast, convinced. When the afflicted girls cried out that there was a yellow bird flying over Goody Cloyse's head, all the people in the meeting house covered their heads for fear of a touch from the invisible yellow bird.

Elizabeth Proctor's examination followed the

same pattern. She was accompanied to the examination by her husband, strong John Proctor. None of the afflicted was able to speak against Goody Proctor. The reason given was that the witches had thrust their hands roughly into the girls' mouths so that they could not make a sound except groans. Only John Indian was capable of speech, and he repeated his former evidence against Goody Cloyse. Mary Warren was oddly silent; there was enough evidence without her.

Elizabeth Proctor turned to the afflicted girls and spoke to them gently. "There is another judgment, dear child," she said to Abigail Williams. But Abigail was staring upward, and Ann Putnam with her. "Look you!" Ann said in a piercing whisper. "There is Goody Proctor, up on the beam!"

Everyone stared frantically upward, and those who sat directly under the beam upon which Goody Proctor was supposedly perched scattered wildly, to get out from under.

John Proctor, standing beside his wife, turned furiously upon the afflicted girls and raised his voice in an angry shout, to say that they were liars and deceivers. When he stopped for a moment, out of breath, Ann Putnam murmured quietly, "Lo! There is Goodman Proctor on the beam by his wife!"

Great cries were raised by all the girls that Goodman Proctor was a wizard. Abigail Williams shouted, "There is Goodman Proctor, going to hurt Goody Bibber!" and Goody Bibber fell rolling onto the floor. Abigail Williams ran forward, raising her hand to strike Goodman Proctor. But when she came near, her hand opened and fell helpless, and she howled that her fingers were burned. Ann Putnam crouched on the floor, staring with wide frightened eyes at Proctor and his wife, and uttering pathetic pleas to them to stop tormenting her. Elizabeth Hubbard sat frozen and helpless in a trance during the whole examination.

If we add to the imagined picture of this scene the shouting and yelling of the audience, with people running back and forth to avoid invisible menaces, benches being overturned, and fainting women and children being hurried out of doors, we can begin to understand the fear that swept the country. No one could think clearly in that bedlam. No one took a moment to reflect that if the afflicted were quieted, the hysteria would stop. It seemed only that the devil and his legions were loose.

Judge Sewall wrote in his diary, of this scene, " 'Twas awful to see how the afflicted persons were agitated." Later, he added in the margin, remorsefully, "Alas, alas, alas!"

The records of these examinations are still in existence, and there is a frightening similarity in the scenes, day after day. Order was never kept in the court, and the judges were almost helpless to control the confusion which broke out whenever the afflicted girls cried out that they were being tormented. The people of Salem Village had never seen a theatrical performance. In fact, all such forms of entertainment were expressly forbidden. So it is not surprising that they flocked to the meeting house for every examination. There they could see a performance which was most certainly never dull.

After the Proctors were sent to prison, Mary Warren apparently had a change of heart. She confessed that she "did but dissemble"; that the actions of herself and the other afflicted children were all pretense. Naturally the others immediately declared that Mary was a witch. She was taken to be held for trial. Even then she said again and again that she had been distracted, and could not now believe that she had committed so cruel a deed as to accuse her benefactors. Nor was that all. She said that the magistrates might just as well have gotten their evidence from a local halfwit "that had been distracted many years, and take notice of what *she* said, as well as any of the afflicted persons."

Mary Warren's examination was a mournful business. She had made a noble attempt to resign from the circle of the afflicted and destroy their power, but there was no one to believe her. The people and the magistrates were only too ready to take it for granted that because of the torments of the witches she had surrendered to them and signed the devil's book. In other words, it was believed that she herself was a witch now, for only a witch would attempt to deny the evidence of the afflicted girls.

When Mary protested her innocence in court, the afflicted girls fell into fits. When Mary, helpless to make the court believe her, burst into tears, the afflicted girls cried out triumphantly that she was afflicted again, because she repented of her witchcraft. "I will speak!" she cried out finally. "Oh, I am sorry for it, I am sorry for it!"

For almost a month Mary remained in confinement in Salem Village, where she could be examined almost daily by Mr. Parris and the magistrates. She was desperately confused by her own position. She believed absolutely that she and the other girls had been deceitful in their torments, and that they had all lied. Yet, when she attempted to tell the judges so, she found that she had proven herself a witch. After thinking the matter over, under Mr. Parris's urging, she finally adopted the only safe way open to her. She confessed fully that she had given in to the witches and had signed the devil's book. She now repented, she said, of her witchcraft. It was the witches who made her swear falsely that the afflicted girls were lying.

Everyone felt very sorry for Mary because she had not been brave enough to resist the tortures of the witches. On the other hand, her confession freed her of all blame, and she meekly took her place again among the afflicted, ready to give further evidence against the Proctors.

Slowly the prisons began to fill with witches. Abigail Hobbs, who wandered the woods at night, eagerly gave even more information than she was asked for and managed to incriminate half a dozen persons, including her own father.

Giles Corey, examined further during these sessions, took a bold stand. He declared himself not guilty. Then one of his neighbors stood up in the meeting house and declared that *he* had heard that Goodman Corey once saw the devil in the shape of a black hog and had been very much frightened. Judge Hathorne turned to Corey and demanded why he had been so frightened, if it was not the devil he saw? Corey drew himself up, angry and defiant, and scowled at the judge.

"Frightened?" he said scornfully. "I do not know that I ever spoke that word in my life." Suspicion of witchcraft he could endure, but not suspicion of cowardice. He refused to speak another word.

Always, just as the pattern began to become monotonous, someone new was found to change the pattern. The examination of Goody Cloyse brought forth the stories of the great meetings of witches. But Abigail Hobbs added a wealth of detail to this bare outline. She testified that the meetings took place in Mr. Parris's pasture, that the witches ate red bread and drank red wine—sometimes blood, but wine when blood was scarce—and listened to long talks delivered by none other than the black man from Boston, assisted now by the "fine, grave" white man. Abigail Hobbs's confession was immediately followed by a similar confession from her mother, who saw the cold eye of suspicion turning upon the whole family. But it was Abigail herself who named and accused her father.

Nehemiah Abbot came up for examination shortly after the Hobbs family was marched off to jail. Goodman Abbot's case is unique. He was the *only* person brought up for examination during this period to be released. During his examination something went very wrong with the spectral evidence. While Goodman Abbot stood nervously on the platform, looking apprehensively from the judges to the afflicted girls and back again, the girls quarreled among themselves. Mercy Lewis said that Goodman Abbot was not the right man. Ann Putnam said yes, he was, too. Mercy said no, he was *not*. Mary Walcott looked at him dubiously, trying to make up her mind. Mercy said Ann could do as she pleased about Goodman Abbot, but he was not the one who was tormenting *her*. Ann had a small fit and said it was caused by Goodman Abbot, who was now sitting on the beam above. Mercy Lewis said no, he was not.

Poor Goodman Abbot, shifting from one foot to another, put in timidly that *he* did not think he was the right one. At last the judges irritably directed that Goodman Abbot be taken outside, where the girls could get a better look at him by daylight. The girls went outside and walked around and around Goodman Abbot, inspecting him carefully and making loud comments upon his personal appearance. Finally, after a great deal of discussion, they agreed. Goodman Abbot had been right all the time. He was innocent.

Mary Easty, sister of Rebecca Nurse and Sarah Cloyse, was accused, examined, and sent to prison. By this time the judges may have begun to wonder at the determination of the afflicted girls against this particular family, and the violent personal hatred still shown by Ann Putnam senior. They questioned the afflicted closely about whether or not they might again be mistaken. The girls refused to change their minds, however, and Mary Easty joined her sisters in prison.

The accusations began to aim higher and wander farther afield. Thomas Putnam, in association with several other prominent citizens of Salem Village, addressed a solemn communication to the judges, telling them that there were rumors of "high and dreadful" evil-doing still to be brought forth. This was certainly true.

Within a day or so a warrant was procured against a Mr. Philip English, a gentleman of wealth and property living in Salem. His wife was also named. The principal evidence against them was supplied by a man who had lost a lawsuit to Mr. English. Mr. and Mrs. English were more fortunate than those accused before them. They were wealthy, and they were members of a social world completely outside the restricted Salem Village limits. They gathered together what money and property they could and escaped to New York. There they stayed until it was considered safe for them to return to Salem. A large part of their property in Salem was stolen while they were gone, but they saved their lives.

Another case resembling that of the Englishes is that of Mr. and Mrs. Cary. The Carys lived in Charlestown and were, like the Englishes, wealthy and prominent people. When the Carys heard that Mrs. Cary had been cried out on in Salem Village as a witch, they were so confident of Mrs. Cary's innocence that they neglected the very practical example set them by the Englishes. In-

stead of staying sensibly in Charlestown, or flee-
ing to the safety of New York, where the Dutch
laughed at witches, the Carys went to Salem Village. They believed that the accusers of Mrs. Cary
would have to proclaim her innocence when she
confronted them. They came to the meeting house
on the twenty-fourth of May and stayed almost
all day, watching the examinations with growing
horror and wondering if they had strayed by some
accident into a madhouse. No one paid any particular attention to them. They noticed that the
afflicted girls were allowed to wander freely
around the meeting house, speaking impudently
to anyone and creating whatever disturbance they
pleased. If they were restrained in any way, they
fell into fits.

After the day's examining was over, Mr. Cary
spoke to one of the officials present, asking if he
might have a few words with the girl who had
accused his wife. Mr. Cary told the official that
he and his wife were most anxious to discover
whether or not the girl had really meant Mrs.
Cary or had confused her with someone else.

Trustingly, Mr. Cary went on to tell the official his name, his address, how he and Mrs. Cary had received word that she had been accused, their trip to Salem Village, and so on. Mr. Cary stated that he and his wife would be waiting at Ingersoll's inn for a quiet word with his wife's accuser, and the official promised to produce her.

Less than an hour later, while Mr. and Mrs. Cary were drinking tea in Ingersoll's inn and listening with fascination to John Indian, who was delivering his regular monologue for visitors, the door of the inn burst open and the whole tumbling, shrieking crew of afflicted girls came in. Howling and yelping, they rolled on the floor, kicked over the table, and smashed the china, blaming it all on Mrs. Cary.

The Carys stood dumbfounded. A warrant for Mrs. Cary's arrest was produced as though by witchcraft. Then it developed that the judges had come along to the inn with the afflicted girls and were even then waiting in another room to conduct a preliminary examination of Mrs. Cary. Mr. and Mrs. Cary had no time to think, much less speak. They were hurried down the hall to the room where the judges were waiting, and Mrs. Cary was found guilty on the spot. John Indian, who not long before had been telling the Carys about the witchcraft, showed up now as a witness against Mrs. Cary, saying that he had known her all the time. He fell into a fit, and the judges, in an effort to bring him out of it, held Mrs. Cary's hand so that she might touch him. John Indian seized her hand and pulled her roughly down onto the floor. Mr. Cary was naturally angered at seeing his wife treated in this fashion, and he leaped forward to defend her, upon which the constables took him by the shoulders and thrust him out of the room. He was forced to wait in the hall while his wife was examined further, and a couple of the afflicted girls, waiting outside, told him that he had better behave or the same would come to him.

Luckily the Carys, although they had behaved foolishly, had influential friends. Mrs. Cary was rescued from prison, much against her will since she still believed that she could stay and prove her innocence. The Carys, like everyone else who could manage it, fled to New York, and while there Mr. Cary wrote a complete account of their treatment in Salem Village. He was astonished to discover that such things could really happen, and he felt that he would not have believed such a story if it had been told to him.

There were people in Massachusetts, many of them in and around Boston, who had distrusted the witchcraft trials from the beginning. Some of these people were clergymen who disapproved of the narrow interpretation of scriptural texts which defined witchcraft. Some were thoughtful persons who could not believe that common justice or humanity would admit the use of spectral evidence against the accused. But most of these people, no matter how enlightened, did not attempt to dispute the existence of witches. Instead they tried, through writing sermons and pamphlets, and using what influence they had, to make sure that the accused people had fair trials upon actual evidence.

Foremost among these enthusiastic workers

was Robert Calef, a Boston businessman of great wit and literary talent. Calef devoted all his energy to the writing of pamphlets which were published and circulated around Boston and, eventually, throughout the whole colony. Calef saw to it that Mr. Cary's account of his adventures in Salem Village was widely read. He also published a good deal of material showing clearly that the use of spectral evidence was against the law, that the statement of an afflicted person that witchcraft was done by an apparition was not admissible as evidence, and that, in any case, the evidence brought forward in Salem Village was imaginary and false. Calef's particular target was Cotton Mather, the colony's main champion against the devil. Calef secretly attended upon one occasion when Mather was engaged in driving out a devil, and he wrote such an unkind and funny account of Mather's operations that for several weeks Mather was too embarrassed to show his face around Boston. As a result, Mather hurried off to Salem Village to get a firsthand report there, and his presence caused a sensation at the trials.

112

It is interesting to note that the afflicted girls in Salem Village cried out upon Robert Calef shortly after Mather's visit. Calef's answer, which reached them with all possible speed, was an announcement of a slander suit for a thousand pounds. The accusation against Calef was immediately withdrawn, and his name was not mentioned again in Salem Village.

But while opposition was beginning to develop slowly, the examinations in Salem Village continued. The high and dreadful things hinted at were coming to pass. The afflicted girls announced that they had identified the person at the heart of the demonic conspiracy. What was more, they named him, to the astonishment and dismay of the entire village. The "black man" was not from Boston, after all. (Perhaps Calef's reaction had warned them.) He was none other than their own former minister, George Burroughs, who had sown this seed in Salem Village before he left them.

A number of people recalled clearly that Burroughs had left the ministry of the village because the people literally starved him out. They refused to pay his fees, and when he found himself penniless, he had been forced to seek a parish elsewhere. When he was at the point of leaving the village, however, the villagers arrested him for overlooking a small bill. Fortunately there were still men in the town brave enough to defend Burroughs, and he was allowed to leave. But he left many enemies behind him, among them the now familiar figures of the Putnam family.

Ann Putnam's evidence against Burroughs was based upon information she said had been given her by the ghosts of his first two wives, both of whom had died in Salem Village. Ann's description of these two ghosts is both horrible and surprising, since both of them died before she was born. Her mother, however, had known both the wives. Both ghosts declared to Ann that they had been murdered by Mr. Burroughs, and showed her great wounds to prove it.

Mr. Burroughs was living in comparative comfort with his third wife in a little village in Maine, where he was known and respected as a conscientious minister. He could not escape the malice of Salem Village, however. When he faced his accusers, it was with dignity, as befitting a minister of the gospel who had spent his life fighting Satan and his devils. But the evidence of the ghosts of his wives was too strong. He was found guilty of murder by witchcraft and identified by all the afflicted as the wizard who presided over the unholy rites in Mr. Parris's pasture.

The heart of the witchcraft conspiracy had been captured. All that now remained was to round up the remaining witches, no matter how many there might be.

Since May of 1692 a new royal governor had been established in Boston. His name was Sir William Phips, and from the very beginning he was helpless before the witchcraft epidemic. The man responsible for his coming to Massachusetts was Increase Mather, father of Cotton Mather, and Sir William arrived to find himself surrounded by influential men who wanted every witch and wizard driven out of New England.

One of Sir William's first acts was to appoint a

special court for the witchcraft trials, without consulting the elected representatives of the people and without giving the situation adequate study. In June the court, composed of learned and prominent men appointed by Sir William, opened at Salem to bring to trial for their lives those witches who had been sent to prison in Boston after preliminary examination.

The trials went much more slowly than the examinations, and with much less sensation. Order was largely maintained in the court, and evidence was given by sworn witnesses rather than by anyone who chose to stand up and make remarks. The results did not differ to any great extent, however. The same type of evidence was entered, by the same people. The judges were as firm as the earlier ones had been in their belief of the guilt of the accused.

When Rebecca Nurse came to trial, after long weeks in prison, the people who knew her were shocked at her condition. She had been old and sick when she was arrested, and all the efforts of her family had been unsuccessful in procuring her any comforts in prison. She was tried for murder by witchcraft, accused of the deaths of two Salem Villagers. At her trial, a written statement was submitted by those who had attended the deathbeds of the two she was supposed to have killed, swearing absolutely that both had died naturally, and not as the result of any witchcraft. The jury, reasonably enough, brought in a verdict of not guilty. The judges sent the jury back to deliberate further, instructing them not to return until they could find Rebecca Nurse guilty of murder by witchcraft. Obediently the jury changed its verdict.

The court trials could not keep pace with the preliminary examinations. More than two hundred people, perhaps as many as three hundred, were in prison awaiting trial. Of these, the ones first tried were almost without exception found guilty. They were not tried in the order in which they had been sent to prison. Little Dorcas Goode, for instance, was never tried at all, although she had spent long months in prison with her mother. Tituba, also, escaped trial, although her final fate is unrecorded. Sarah Goode, Rebecca Nurse, the Proctors, and George Burroughs were all tried and found guilty. In the cases of the Proctors and Rebecca Nurse, the court and jury deliberately ignored lengthy and sincere petitions for their release signed by influential friends and well-wishers and testifying to an absolute belief in their innocence.

Cotton Mather was present at the trial of George Burroughs and was much gratified at the stern and unyielding determination of the judges.

Martha Corey was tried and found guilty. Her husband, Giles Corey, took a sterner course. He knew that convicted witches and wizards forfeited their property to the government. He knew, too, that he was no wizard, and he scorned to be tried in public shame. Moreover, he had been angered to such a degree that he felt it beneath him to answer the questions asked him. He therefore refused to speak at all. When he was called into court, he could not be brought to say either "Guilty" or "Not guilty." He stood mute, and no questioning or threat could shake him. It was therefore not possible to bring him to trial, and although the punishment for his actions was, legally, that he be put to death, Corey knowingly chose that way. Because of that, his property went without hindrance to his sons. But his attitude in court and even his death showed clearly to all of New England the contempt he felt for his accusers. His courage and pride made him something of a popular hero, in spite of the taint of witchcraft, and people on their way to court to see the witches tried sang snatches of ballads praising Giles Corey.

Meanwhile, the afflicted girls were quite busy. Two of them (their names are unrecorded) had been sent for by a citizen of Andover. His wife was sadly ailing, and he hoped that the bewitched girls from Salem Village might be able to see if she suffered from the malice of a witch. Both the husband and the rest of the people in Andover had good cause to regret this rash act. The afflicted girls declared eagerly that there was indeed witchcraft in Andover, and they guaranteed to find out the witch or witches. One shortsighted

Andover resident suggested that it might be a good idea if all the Andover women, rich or poor, respectable or not, godly or otherwise, lined up to be reviewed by the afflicted girls. Accordingly, the women of Andover presented themselves so that the girls could "see" the witches. It came as a great shock to everyone, and particularly the women, when the girls confidently identified nearly everyone as guilty. The Andover magistrate signed forty warrants and then threw down his pen, declaring he had done enough and would arrest no more. The girls at once turned upon him, and he and his family had to flee for their lives.

The Andover witches joined the Salem Village witches in prison. By this time all the prisons in Salem, Ipswich, Boston, and Cambridge were sadly overcrowded.

By September 22, 1692, Giles Corey and nineteen other persons had been executed publicly. There is no way of knowing the numbers who died in prison. The nineteen who were hanged on Gallows Hill outside Salem were:

BRIDGET BISHOP	JOHN WILLARD
SARAH GOODE	MARTHA CARRIER
SARAH WILDES	MARTHA COREY
ELIZABETH HOW	MARY EASTY
SUSANNA MARTIN	ALICE PARKER
REBECCA NURSE	ANN PUDEATOR
GEORGE BURROUGHS	MARGARET SCOTT
JOHN PROCTOR	WILMOT REED
GEORGE JACOBS, SR.	SAMUEL WARDWELL
MARY PARKER	

Elizabeth Proctor was condemned to death, but reprieved. Sarah Osburn is known to have died in prison.

Not one person who confessed to practicing witchcraft was executed. The persons executed were those who insisted upon their innocence. Giles Corey was ordered pressed to death by heavy stones for refusing to speak at all. His execution may have marked a turning point in the witchcraft epidemic.

121

6

THE DEVIL DEPARTS

On September 22, 1692, the day of the last execution, the witchcraft delusion began to disappear. No one realized it at first. The afflicted girls continued crying out upon anyone within reach, the preliminary examinations continued, and the prisons stayed crowded. The special court in Salem adjourned, to meet again in two or three weeks and resume the trials. A change had taken place, however, in the feelings of the people. Perhaps it was due to the courage of Giles Corey. Perhaps everyone was growing weary of supernatural terrors. Perhaps the change was due to the deplorable condition of the colony in general. Perhaps it was a combination of all these things. In any case, a slow change of opinion took place. People simply stopped believing that their friends and neighbors were witches.

The accusations had grown almost frenzied, and Judge Corwin, who had never pursued the examinations with the enthusiasm shown by Judge Hathorne, began to show distinct signs of leniency. The girls immediately cried out that he was trying to protect his mother-in-law, a gentle old lady who lived in the highest Boston society. The girls said she was a witch, and that she tormented them. No one believed them, and Judge Corwin became even more doubtful of witchcraft accusations. The girls cried out, then, against a prominent minister who had publicly rebuked them, and Judge Hathorne told them sharply that they were mistaken. The wife of Sir William Phips, the royal governor, was accused, and the accusation was ignored. The girls cried out on Mrs. Hale, the generous and beloved wife of an important clergyman. Mr. Hale had been one of the most enthusiastic hunters of witches, and had done much to further the investigations and trials. When, however, his own wife was accused, he perceived that he had long been in error, and he repudiated the afflicted girls and their evidence.

Other incidents followed, showing that the tide had turned. The afflicted girls, being taken for a walk one September afternoon, met an old woman on a bridge who would not let them cross. Irked, they fell into fits, screaming that the old woman was a witch who meant to hold them there forever. The old woman looked at them coldly and walked away, passersby turned their heads to look at something else, and the girls got up sheepishly and went on with their walk.

Then, from Andover, came word that half a dozen actions for slander had been started against the accusers. The doctrine of "spectral evidence" became suddenly an extraordinarily unpopular one to hold. The special court was dissolved altogether and a new one established. This court, which met at Salem in January 1693, began to release prisoners with unusual speed. The new court included all of the judges who had formerly been on the special court, but it did not admit spectral evidence. As a result, in a series of trials lasting through the spring of 1693, no one was found guilty. At last, in May of that year, Sir William ran out of patience and issued a proclamation discharging all the witches left in jail. This proclamation released one hundred and fifty people.

Once the epidemic was over, the people of Massachusetts could sit back and try to estimate the damage done. Twenty innocent people had been executed, and others had died in jail. Those acquitted and released by proclamation could not be set free until they had paid jail and court fees, as well as board for the whole time of their imprisonment. As a result, some of these unfortunate people had to stay on in jail because they could not pay their way out, and some of them were utterly impoverished by the payment of their prison fees.

Many people of wealth, fame, and influence had fled to other colonies to escape unjust accusation. Most of these people showed no desire to return. Their Massachusetts property had in most cases been confiscated and dishonorably plundered, their reputations injured, and their loyalty to Massachusetts hopelessly destroyed.

The property of all the accused had been seized, sometimes with shocking haste, sometimes illegally, by dishonest officials. The heirs of many of those who died filed claims for restoration, but few received anything. Suits were brought by those released, in a vain attempt to recover property taken or wantonly destroyed by court officials; but few of these received anything. Many of those who had suffered so severely and unjustly left the colony forever and made no secret of their resentment.

The whole colony, moreover, had suffered. The people had been so determined upon hunting out and destroying witches that they had neglected everything else. Planting, cultivating, the care of houses, barns, roads, fences, were all forgotten. As a direct result, food became scarce and taxes higher. Farms were mortgaged or sold, first to pay prison fees, then to pay taxes; frequently they were abandoned. Salem Village began that slow decay which eventually erased its houses and walls, but never its name and memory.

The afflicted girls retired abruptly from public life. The suits against them were allowed to lapse, and the girls endeavored to settle down quietly as private citizens. We do not know what happened to most of them. Later documents indicate, however, that some of the girls ended their lives in disgrace and poverty. The elder Ann Putnam died not long after her victims. The younger Ann Putnam lived quietly on in Salem Village, a semi-invalid. She brought up her younger brothers and sisters after the death of her parents, and in the year 1706, before a great audience in the meeting house of Salem Village, she was received to Communion upon the reading of a public confession. Part of her confession says: "I desire to be hum-

bled before God . . . that I . . . should . . . be made
an instrument for the accusing of several persons
of a grievous crime, whereby their lives were taken
away from them, whom now I have just grounds
and good reason to believe they were innocent
persons." She particularly asked pardon of the
Nurse family, which had suffered so cruelly at
her hands. Samuel Nurse, as representative of the
family, accepted her confession, and Ann Putnam
was admitted to Communion. She died ten years
later.

Little Elizabeth Parris completely regained her
health after a year spent in a wholesome atmos-
phere, living with relatives in Boston and playing
with her noisy, unimaginative cousins. Her father
was not so fortunate. Much of the shameful conduct of the witchcraft examinations was attrib-
uted to him, and he was held by the villagers to
be largely responsible for the innocent people who
suffered. He was driven from the parish after another year or so spent quarreling with his congregation, and he spent the rest of his life in
obscure poverty. His house in Salem Village is

nothing now but barren ground and the only record of him is in the story of the witchcraft epidemic.

Jonathan Corwin rose in importance and wealth, although never free from the reputation of the witchcraft trials. John Hathorne never conceded that he had been mistaken, and persisted all his life in maintaining that the witches were guilty, and that the part he had acted was honorable. One hundred and fifty years later a descendant of John Hathorne's wrote *The House of the Seven Gables*—the story, in part, of a cruel man who had helped to bring witches to execution, and who died with the memory heavy on his conscience. In this story Nathaniel Hawthorne (the *w* had been added somewhere along the way) adapted the dying words of Sarah Goode, who stood on the scaffold and shouted at the clergyman who begged her to confess, "I am no more a witch than you are a wizard, and if you take away my life, God will give you blood to drink!" Unlike his ancestor, Nathaniel Hawthorne thought the witchcraft fever was "a terrible delusion."

For many years a day of general fasting—of remorse and repentance for the evil of the witch-craft days—was observed in Massachusetts. For the rest of his life, Judge Sewall observed this day as one, also, of personal humiliation, and was accustomed to beg public prayers for himself to avert divine justice from him. His diary shows that after thirty years he was still attempting to atone for what he regarded as a mortal error.

In 1696 a document had been presented to the public, signed with the names of twelve men who had served as jurors in several Salem witchcraft cases. This document included these final apologetic words:

"We do therefore hereby signify to all in general (and to the surviving sufferers in special) our deep sense of, and sorrow for, our errors, in acting on such evidence to the condemning of any person; and do hereby declare, that we justly fear that we were sadly deluded and mistaken . . .

"We do heartily ask forgiveness of you all, whom we have justly offended; and do declare, according to our present minds, we would none of us do such things again on such grounds for the whole world; praying you to accept of this in way of satisfaction for our offense, and that you would bless the inheritance of the Lord, that he may be entreated for the land."

On March 5, 1954, a New York newspaper announced that six of the women hanged as witches in 1692 had been cleared by the lower house of the Massachusetts legislature. But not until 1957 did the Commonwealth of Massachusetts officially clear the names of everyone who had been accused of witchcraft.

Although the Massachusetts witchcraft epidemic is a shameful chapter in our history, it had, strangely enough, some good results. For several reasons, Massachusetts is unique in the history of witchcraft. The later trials were the first in which spectral evidence was not allowed. The epidemic in Massachusetts lasted for sixteen months, and then stopped absolutely. After the last witches died on Gallows Hill in 1692, there was never another execution for witchcraft in New England.

The judges and jurors in Massachusetts were the only ones in the history of witchcraft trials to admit publicly that they had been wrong and unjust.

This public recantation of the judges and jurors did a great deal to lessen the enormous hold which witchcraft and sorcery had held for so long. People who had been writing and arguing that witches did not exist found support in the fact that the very people who had condemned the witches no longer believed in their guilt. Moreover, once people started doubting that the devil had his converts, it was possible to begin to believe that the devil was not an actuality, walking the earth with his demons.

Although there were witchcraft trials and executions in England for a dozen years longer, and for as long as a hundred years more in some parts of Europe, Massachusetts had taken the first step to end the persecution. The state and its citizens had shown that although they had acted in panic, they were honestly prepared to confess their error and make what restitution they could. Moreover, they had demonstrated that spectral evidence, guilt by association, and a belief that the prisoner was guilty before she or he was tried, are not means to be used in fighting any evil, no matter how frightening it may seem.

AFTERWORD

It is difficult to understand the seeming madness that swept Salem Village in 1692 without an understanding of the many factors which had been building for long centuries before. Since the establishment of the Christian church, a surprising amount of study and scholarship had been devoted to learning about its enemies. For nearly seventeen centuries before Salem Village was born, learned men had been endeavoring to control witchcraft.

Naturally, religious people at that time were anxious to determine the extent to which their church was menaced by supernatural powers. Everyone believed that there actually was a devil, a created being whose efforts were directed toward the working of evil. It was important to know precisely how effective the devil could be, and, of course, how best to fight against him.

The devil was believed to carry on his war against heaven through the use of human beings. Every person won to his service was a blow against heaven and the strength of the church. It was commonly believed that the devil worked in person among mankind, using all his weapons to urge humanity to his side. He could tempt weak souls with visions of wealth, power, and success. He could trick people and lie to them, and he could even endow some with his own supernatural abilities enabling them to work magic. He was assisted by numbers of demons, all of whom were subordinate to their master, but who were all permitted to transact bargains and enroll humanity among their numbers.

The amount of careful study given to the habits and powers of the devil and his army is astonishing. For instance, in the middle sixteenth century a French scholar announced triumphantly that after years of painstaking labor he had discovered the precise number of the demonic army. There were, he said, 7,409,127 demons, commanded by 79 infernal princes who were responsible only to Satan himself. This figure was indignantly denied about ten years later by another French scholar, who insisted that there were actually only 7,405,920 demons, commanded by only 72 princes. A year or so later, still another scholar entered the discussion. He explained that he had discovered the basic arrangement of the demonic army. It was divided into legions, cohorts, companies, and individuals, and these forces totaled slightly more than the population of the world. There was, in fact, one and a fraction demons for each member of the human race.

Each of these demons has a name, most of

them brought to light by equally earnest scholars. As late as the end of the seventeenth century an English student published careful portraits of half a dozen of the chief demons. They were sketched, he said, from life. They are not an attractive-looking group.

There are also many specimens of demonic handwriting. One of them, signed by the demon Asmodeus, is so badly misspelled that it is almost unreadable. This was explained by pointing out that it was not necessary for a demon to learn to spell. His job was to torment mankind.

Prominent religious people frequently had conversations with Satan and with demons. They argued difficult religious questions, and the demons were considered excellent in debate, although not always truthful. There were many magical ways of summoning demons, although the use of such magic was expressly forbidden by both religious and civil law.

The demons were able to appear without being summoned, but they could not harm anyone so long as the proper religious protection against them was observed. They could, however, enter into the body of a human being and control it. This, called "possession," was a frequent occurrence even as late as the end of the seventeenth century. The victim who was possessed would behave wildly and utterly without reason, shout out curses and blasphemies, and sometimes even endanger the lives of others. It required all the force of religious power to drive out the demon, and many important churchmen spent long hours in argument, persuasion, and prayer, mocked and abused by a demon who refused to leave a victim's body.

The great work of the devil lay among the simple people, who did not care for religious argument and believed only that one had to be very careful to stay out of the clutches of the devil. They did not care to know the precise numbers of the legions of the devil. A man who harvested a good crop gave thanks to heaven for its blessings. When his barn burned, and his crop with it, he could only see that it was the devil's work.

The devil's methods were simple. He, or one of

his demons, approached a human being with offers which were made as appealing as possible. If the victim was poor, he was offered vast wealth. If he was dissatisfied, he was offered power, love, or magical abilities.

These temptations often proved so irresistible that the victim agreed to forsake his church and become a member of the devil's "church." He was then given a devil's mark, a demonic agent, or familiar, who might seem to others to be only an ordinary cat, dog, or bird, but who was actually an evil being. The familiar was both a servant and a spy. He performed whatever evil he was ordered to do, but reported back to the devil regularly.

Once the victim had been fully initiated into his position as a follower of the devil, he was known as a "witch" or a "wizard." It is usual to think of women as witches and men as wizards. However, there is no sharp distinction, and the records show that the words were often used interchangeably.

The witch, who had bartered any hope of

heaven in exchange for the devil's offer, found usually that the devil was a liar and a trickster. Vast wealth turned out to be a few cents, great power was only the delusion of madness.

But the witch was believed to have certain powers of magic. He or she could raise storms, start fires, cause sickness by the glance of an eye or the touch of a hand. He or she could harm humans and animals, and kill them if he or she chose. He or she could destroy crops and cause hallucinations. In addition, the witch could remove any spell he or she had cast and was able to heal sickness. Some witches preferred petty irritations. One English witch customarily sent a plague of fleas to any person who offended her. The witches were supposed to have control of poison, and it was a usual thing for wealthy and important people to call in a witch when an enemy needed destroying.

Witches were thought to be afraid of water and, naturally, of any true religious thing. Although they sometimes came to church in order to avoid suspicion, the church service was uncomfortable for them, and they sometimes secretly mocked the words and gestures. A witch was not able to pray. One of the great tests of witchcraft was to require the witch to say the Lord's Prayer. In demonic rites it was said backward, and a witch could not, however he or she tried, say it correctly. Many unfortunate people proved to the judges that they were witches simply because, during an examination, they became so frightened that they got the words confused.

By the end of the eighteenth century more than two million people of the "civilized" world had been executed for witchcraft.

In England the laws against witchcraft had become progressively more severe. In 1542, under English law, it was a crime to use "witchcraftes enchauntementes or sorceries." In 1563, under Queen Elizabeth, a new Parliamentary act made the practice of witchcraft a crime punishable by exposure in the pillory for a first offense and punishable by death for a second offense.

When James I succeeded Elizabeth, however, his own superstition and fear produced an increase in general alarm over the subject. James wrote and published a treatise on witchcraft called *Demonologie*. It condemned the practice of witchcraft in all its forms and argued that only the most severe laws could restrain the witches. Thus, in 1604, the English Parliament under James passed a new act, making any practice of witchcraft punishable by death for a first offense. This law was in effect when the Puritans came to Massachusetts.

The Massachusetts colony was established during the period when witchcraft in England was one of the great topics of the day. Although the Puritans insisted that they had left England because of the oppressive nature of the English church, they did not want *liberty* of religion, but only conformity. They in turn persecuted all who differed from themselves in belief, and drove from their colony anyone who refused to accept their strict ways.

Just as the Puritans adopted a more stern view of religion, so their ideas about the devil became narrower. They saw the devil still as the enemy of mankind, but they thought that he was also the particular, personal enemy of the Puritans. They thought that since their religion was the truest, the devil was most anxious to destroy it.

Each individual among the Puritans felt that he was called upon to fight the devil personally. Also, they believed that most people outside the Puritan faith were helping the devil's cause because they were not strict enough. They knew that many people who believed themselves to be devout Christians nevertheless broke many religious laws and treated their religion carelessly. To the Puritans, neglect of their religion meant neglect of their whole pattern of life. The religious framework was the base of all their government and all their efforts to start a new home in Massachusetts.

In addition to religious fervor and intolerance, the isolation of Salem Village, the feuds between jealous villagers and wealthy landowning farmers, and the drabness of their everyday lives all seem to have contributed to the unique "witch hunt" of 1692. Psychologists have pointed out that there is such a thing as contagious hysteria. Groups of people can "infect" one another and copy one another's symptoms. This kind of behavior is often caused by extreme fear or guilt such as the girls must have been suffering from dabbling in forbidden "magic" with Tituba.

In recent years scientists have even come up with the theory that the "afflicted children" may have eaten contaminated bread. A fungus called ergot sometimes infects the rye grain used in bread-making. This fungus can cause dizziness, headaches, and hallucinations. It is thought possible that the local grain crop may have contained this fungus in 1692. So far, however, this theory has not achieved wide acceptance.

Relive history!

Turn the page for more great books . . .

Landmark Books® Grades 6 and Up

Landmark Books® Grades 2 and Up

 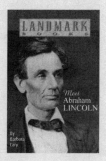 

Landmark Books® Grades 4 and Up

And coming soon: